FUGITIVE P1

Miniature portrait of James Edward Austen-Leigh, c.1818,
watercolour and pencil.

*(Reproduced by kind permission of a descendant of James Edward Austen-Leigh;
photo reproduced by kind permission of the Hampshire Record Office.)*

Fugitive Pieces

Trifles light as Air

The poems of

JAMES EDWARD AUSTEN-LEIGH

Nephew and biographer of Jane Austen

Edited with an Introduction and Notes by

DAVID SELWYN

THE JANE AUSTEN SOCIETY

The Jane Austen Society

First published in Great Britain 2006
by the Jane Austen Society
c/o 22 Hyde Street
Winchester
SO23 7DR

ISBN 0 9538174 6 6

Printed by Sarsen Press
Winchester. SO23 7DR

CONTENTS

Preface	page vii.
Introduction	1
A note on the text	6
The Neck of Veal	7
To Papa with a Knife	8
To Mamma	9
The Patriot	10
The Races	12
Fox hunting commenced	13
On the Dummer Harriers	14
Dirt & slime	17
Address to Buonaparte	19
The School-boys wish	20
To Anna, A riddle	21
To Anna	22
The flower. To Anna on her birthday	23
Ode of Horace imitated	25
To Miss J Austen	27
The Lion & the Fox	28
On the death of L B Wither Esqre.	29
To Manydown	31
To Miss C. Craven	33
To Mrs B. Lefroy. On her Wedding day	36
A Letter to Miss Caroline Austen	38
On Westminster Abbey	40
The Wood walk ... To Anna	43
To Caroline on her birthday	45
On the defeat of Buonaparte at Waterloo	47
The Heroes	49
Epitaph on old Justice	50
Ulisses announces to Hecuba that the Manes of Achilles demand the death of Polixena	52

To Mamma   53

Moses   54

Verses to the Memory of Miss Jane Austen   58

Letter to Mrs B. Lefroy. Wyards. After a Basingstoke Ball   62

To the Memory of the Revd James Austen   64

Lines to Dyce written 1821   65

A letter from an Undergraduate to his Friend, descriptive of   67
    the late Commemoration

'Mirror of Life'   73

Lines accompanying a pearl pin, addressed to William Heathcote   74

Prologue to The Sultan   76

An Epilogue to the Sultan   77

Lines written at Bear hill Cottage, Berkshire   79

On a run from Milk hill   81

Prologue spoken by Edward in the character of 'Scrub of the
    Company'   83

Œnigma written at Chawton in the summer 1820   85

Enigma   86

Charades   87

Bouts-Rimés   91

Noun Verses   96

Bibliography   101

Notes   103

Index of first lines   137

PREFACE

It is not widely known that Jane Austen's nephew James Edward Austen-Leigh, like so many members of the talented Austen family, and indeed like Jane Austen herself, wrote poetry. This is because, with the exception of the verse he wrote in astonishment at finding out that his aunt was a published author, which is occasionally quoted in biographies, virtually nothing appeared in print until the very small selection (only three poems, in fact) that I was able to include in *Jane Austen Collected Poems and verse of the Austen family* (1996). The discovery of a manuscript album of his verses in the collection at Isel Hall, however, together with a scrapbook containing some of his charming silhouette pictures, suggested the present publication. I have included all the other poems by him that I have been able to trace, though I suspect that there are more that have not come to light; I have omitted only one, in Latin, and nine hymns which would not have added to the gaiety of the volume.

I am very grateful to Mary Burkett for allowing me to publish the text of the Isel album and the silhouettes, and for the warm welcome she has given me on the many occasions when I have worked on them at Isel Hall. David Gilson has been equally generous and hospitable in respect of the manuscripts in his possession; and the staff of the Hampshire Record Office in Winchester, where most of the other poems are to be found, have been, as always, unfailingly helpful and kind. Other individuals, libraries and institutions on whose assistance I have relied, and to whom I owe a debt of gratitude, include the British Library; Cambridge University Library; Tom Carpenter and the Trustees of the Jane Austen Memorial Trust; Ann Channon; Janet Clarke; Barbara Croucher; Derrick Gale and colleagues at Bristol Grammar School; Ian Gilmour; Tony Hill and the staff at Sarsen Press; the Committee of the Jane Austen Society; Maggie Lane; Deirdre Le Faye; Helen Lefroy; the late Derek Lucas; Brian Southam; Michael Warman; Lesley Wilson; the staff of Winchester Reference Library.

DAVID SELWYN

INTRODUCTION

To most readers of Jane Austen, James Edward Austen-Leigh is best known as the author of the first biography of her, the *Memoir* of 1870, while those familiar with her letters will remember him as the charming and good-looking nephew of whom she and Cassandra were so fond. Knowing her well in his childhood – he was already eighteen when she died in July 1817 – when she was still an entirely private person, he lived through the period of her growing fame until the time came when it was obvious from public requests for information about her that a fuller account of her life was required than her brother Henry had been able to provide in the 'Biographical Notice' attached to the first edition of *Northanger Abbey* and *Persuasion* and enlarged in 1833. But the *Memoir of Jane Austen* was not his only literary work. In 1865 he published *Recollections of the Early Days of the Vine Hunt*, an account of the men who hunted the north Hampshire countryside in the period of his youth and later, with amusing stories of days in the field and affectionate character sketches of some of the Austens' friends and neighbours. Though it appeared anonymously (the title page simply bore the phrase 'by a sexagenarian'), it is a very personal book, informed by both a relish for the sport and a gentle humour that are entirely characteristic of its author.

James Edward was the only member of Jane Austen's family circle, apart, of course, from herself, to publish anything substantial in his own lifetime (though at Oxford her brothers James and Henry had edited a periodical, *The Loiterer*, to which they both contributed papers); but the aunt's example was too strong to be resisted, and he and his sisters all attempted to write novels in their youth – Jane Austen described part of his, after hearing him read it, as 'extremely clever; written with great ease & spirit'. Indeed, many of the Austens wrote at one time or another, for the most part verses for private amusement. Mrs Austen was particularly adept at these, and such as have survived show her to have been genuinely resourceful and witty. Meanwhile James was the author of a number of poems, some humorous, some serious, which, though no attempt ever seems to have been made to publish them in his lifetime, were quite ambitious in scope. It is not surprising then that his son, James Edward, should have acquired the habit of verse writing from an early age, and in his comic pieces at least – the enigmas, charades, bouts-rimés and noun verses that constituted popular games of the day among lively-minded people – he demonstrated a sure touch. Most of the verses that have come to light were written in his youth and addressed to his parents, his sisters or his friends, since, like his father, he was fond of writing affectionately to those nearest to him (though without his father's tendency to sermonise); later ones were intended to amuse his own children, who were also encouraged to write. He was less concerned than James

Austen with depicting the beauties of the countryside, despite being an equally accomplished artist, as his drawings and silhouettes show; but he shared with him a capacity for turning his hand to writing prologues and epilogues for private theatrical entertainments, as the occasion demanded. It is reasonable to assume that some of his youthful verses would have been read at Chawton Cottage, and no doubt the astonishment he expressed in the one addressed to his aunt on discovering that she was an illustrious author would have been much enjoyed.

James Edward Austen-Leigh (always known in the family as Edward) was born in the rectory at Deane in Hampshire on 17 November 1798, the second child of the Revd James Austen, who was curate to his father, the Revd George Austen. James Austen's eldest child, Jane Anna Elizabeth, had been born five years earlier to his first wife, Anne Mathew, who died in 1795; James subsequently married Mary Lloyd, by whom he had, as well as James Edward, a daughter, Caroline Mary Craven, in 1805. When Mr Austen retired to Bath in 1801 with Mrs Austen, Cassandra and Jane, James became his curate at Steventon and moved his family to the rectory there; and on his father's death in January 1805 he succeeded him as rector. Though it seems that Mrs James Austen was not close to her stepdaughter, James Edward was very fond of Anna, as several of his poems to her testify. He was a warm-hearted boy, with an affectionate nature and a lively sense of humour; and as he grew up these qualities developed, Jane Austen writing of him at the age of eighteen, 'He grows still, & still improves in appearance, at least in the estimation of his Aunts, who love him better & better, as they see the sweet temper & warm affection of the Boy confirmed in the young Man'.[1]

Between August 1812 and June 1813 James Edward attended a preparatory school in Ramsbury, Wiltshire run by the Revd Edward Graves Meyrick, where William Heathcote, son of Jane and Cassandra's friend Elizabeth Bigg, was already a pupil. Then, in the autumn of 1814, following the abandonment of a plan for him to go to Eton, he began at Winchester College, where William also went. Two years later he entered Exeter College, Oxford, obtaining a Craven Founder's Kin Scholarship, and he was there when first his aunt and then his father died in respectively 1817 and 1819. Jane's brother Henry held the living of Steventon for three years until his nephew William Knight was ready to take it, and Mary and Caroline were obliged to leave the rectory. Over a number of years they took a series of rented houses near Newbury, settling in Newtown in 1825 and then in 1836 moving to Speen, where Mary died in 1843.

When he left Oxford James Edward made up his mind to be a clergyman, despite opposition from his great-aunt, Mrs Leigh-Perrot, from whom he stood to inherit his late great-uncle's estate, Scarlets. Having been ordained in London on 1 June 1823 by the Bishop of Winchester, he became curate at

Newtown and lived there with his mother and sister, leading a very busy social life, dining out and attending balls. He also fished, but his favourite occupation was hunting, which at this period he engaged in three times a week during the season. He hunted principally with the Vine, whose Master, William Chute, was an old friend of the Austens; and it was at the Chutes' house, The Vyne, near Basingstoke, that he met his future wife, Emma Smith, second daughter of Mrs Chute's widowed sister Augusta. Mrs Chute wrote of him appreciatively to Emma: 'he certainly is a very agreeable companion, cheerful, lively, animated, ready to converse, willing to read out loud, never in the way and just enough of poetry and romance to please me and yet not to overlook sober reason'.[2] They were married on 16 December 1828 at Tring in Hertfordshire, and the first five years of their marriage were spent with the rest of the Smith family at Tring Park. Mrs Leigh-Perrot thoroughly approved of the marriage and decided once and for all to make James Edward her heir.

In November 1833 they left Tring, with their three children, and took a house in Speen. James Edward was already suffering from a throat complaint that meant that he was unable to officiate in church, or indeed to read aloud at all. The condition lasted several years, imposing upon him a protracted period of inactivity that was most uncongenial to a man of his natural energy. He occupied himself with his family, to which two more boys were added while they were at Speen. He also employed his time in making silhouette pictures, as his daughter Mary Augusta describes in her *Memoir* of him:

> He took to a new occupation, which he carried to great perfection. This was cutting out figures and scenes from natural life in black paper. As a boy he had been accustomed to cut out and paint packs of hounds, printing their names on the blank side, and the first time his sister Caroline, when a little girl, saw a real pack of hounds assembled she ran round to look for their names on their other side. The packs of hounds continued to be cut out in later life for his children's benefit, but the black paper figures belong entirely to his years of illness. He was taught this art by Miss Clinton – a relation of Mr. Majendie [the vicar of Speen] – who came to visit at the vicarage. He never drew his pictures, but cut them out by eye, and they are wonderful for their accuracy, grace, variety, and observation of nature. I never saw or heard of any like them. Miss Clinton's were confined to a few half-classical figures, but our father took his subjects from natural objects. He used special scissors, the points being about an inch long, and the curved handles about three inches. These and a sheet of black paper were his only tools. A few of his groups were placed on screens or a cabinet of white wood and then varnished, but the greater number are preserved in a book. He dropped this art entirely after he recovered from his illness.[3]

His recovery was complete by the time of Mrs Leigh-Perrot's death in November 1836 and he and Emma took possession of Scarlets in the following January, their house in Speen being taken over by Mary and Caroline. James Edward had also inherited money from his great-uncle and under the terms of his will he was obliged to add Leigh to his own name. For the next fifteen years he remained at Scarlets, improving the house and gardens, adding to his family (five further children were born there), encouraging the boys to hunt, and doing duty at nearby Knowl Hill, where he had helped to build a church. It was as a result of his efforts in the latter work that he was offered the remunerative living of Bray, where in April 1853 the family moved. Over a period of time he restored the church and built three others in the widely scattered parish. Scarlets was let until 1863, when he sold it to the tenant in order to buy his eldest son, Cholmeley, a partnership in the publishing firm of Spottiswoode & Co; he had never cared as much for the house he inherited as for the one in which he had grown up and it seems that leaving it caused him few regrets.

Both at Scarlets and at Bray there were family entertainments, the acting of charades being a particular favourite. They also played the kind of written games, often in verse, that had been handed down from James Edward's parents' and grandparents' generations: examples of riddles, enigmas, bouts-rimés and noun verses exist by both himself and his children, But literary activity of a more sustained kind was undertaken by James Edward, first in 1865 with *the Recollections of the Early Days of the Vine Hunt*, and then five years later with the *Memoir of Jane Austen*, for which he solicited help from other members of the Austen family, who provided him with letters and manuscripts. It was so successful that a year later, in the summer of 1871, he brought out a second edition, in which he included the cancelled chapter of *Persuasion,* an early little play, 'The Mystery', *Lady Susan* and the fragment which he called *The Watsons,* as well as a summary of *Sanditon*. With some of the money he received for the book he erected the brass memorial tablet to his aunt in Winchester Cathedral. It is no exaggeration to say that, with its personal memories and first-hand knowledge of its subject, the *Memoir* has been the basis of all subsequent lives of Jane Austen.

James Edward died after a short illness at Bray Vicarage on 8 September 1874 in his seventy-sixth year, followed by Emma two years later and his sister Caroline in 1880, Anna having died in 1872. The biographical pursuit he had initiated was followed by several of his descendants. Mary Augusta wrote not only the *Memoir* of her father but also *Personal Aspects of Jane Austen;* and his youngest son William collaborated with a cousin, Montagu George Knight, on *Chawton Manor and its Owners* and with his nephew Richard Arthur Austen-Leigh on *Jane Austen, her Life and Letters, a Family Record.* Richard Arthur Austen-Leigh, Cholmeley's second son, did a great deal of work on the family archive and published several books, including *Pedigree of Austen* and *Austen Papers;* and a daughter of Cholmeley, Emma Austen-Leigh, wrote *Jane Austen and Steventon* and *Jane Austen and Bath.* Thus James Edward can truly be said to have occupied a central position in the literary history of the Austen family.

The poems, mostly written in his youth, while obviously not of as great importance as the *Memoir* of his aunt, offer a view of people and places that she knew; and some of the earlier ones would almost certainly have been read by her. By the time he began writing about life in and around Steventon, she had long left it, and she must have enjoyed reading about such favourite places of her childhood as the paths near the church or the wood walk by the rectory garden. She would have appreciated too that he shared many of her literary tastes. We can assume in him a knowledge of the poets that both she and James read – Shakespeare, of course, Milton and, closer to his own time, Thomson, Cowper, Crabbe, Southey and Scott; and naturally he would have been well versed in Classical literature, particularly Homer, Greek tragedy, Virgil and Horace. He would also have been familiar with the large amount of verse regularly published in periodicals, most notably *The Gentleman's Magazine,* which reflected on the affairs of the day; its influence on him can be seen in poems such as 'The Heroes' and the 'Address to Buonaparte'.

There is no doubt that the poems of both James Edward and his father were circulated among the family. All three of James Austen's children made copies of his poetry; Emma Smith read some of it before her marriage and wrote to Caroline 'I admire extremely your Father's poetry it shows what a sweet & elegant mind his was & you may well be proud of it & him'.[4] Caroline was proud of her father's poetry, and so was her brother; and it is clear that they were both inspired by his example to write verse themselves. Caroline later destroyed most of hers, but it is fortunate that James Edward's was preserved, some of it in copies but much of it in his own hand. Many of the poems written in childhood and up to the time he left Oxford are found in two small notebooks, 'Fugitive Pieces' and 'Fugitive Pieces 2nd', to which he gave the subtitle 'Trifles light as air'. The very fact that he collected his work in book form and set it out with Contents pages (which do not entirely correspond with the actual contents of the volumes) shows him to be making the same engagement with published literature that Jane Austen made in the elaborate titles and dedications of the Juvenilia. *Fugitive Pieces* was a well-used title for volumes of poetry in the eighteenth and nineteenth centuries, and is found in the work of more than twenty poets, among them Byron, following the publication of a book of that name by Horace Walpole in 1758; James Edward probably came across it in the two-volume anthology brought out by Dodsley in 1761 (reprinted 1771), *Fugitive Pieces on various subjects by several authors.* It could be said that his pieces were more fugitive than most; but while perhaps no very great claims can be made for them as poetry, their value lies in their considerable biographical interest, besides the undoubted pleasure that they give. Above all, their humour, tenderness and gentle wisdom unmistakably convey the personality of a good and kindly man who was loved and valued by his family and to whom all readers of Jane Austen have reason to be grateful.

Notes

1 *Jane Austen's Letters*, 3rd edn, ed. Deirdre Le Faye (Oxford, 1996), p. 327.
2 Quoted in Mary Augusta Austen Leigh, *James Edward Austen Leigh: A Memoir* (privately printed, 1911), p. 41.
3 Ibid., pp. 70-71.
4 Letter of 5 November [1828], HRO 23M93/66/2.

A NOTE ON THE TEXT

The poems in this volume are printed wherever possible from James Edward Austen-Leigh's own manuscripts; if no autograph exists but there is more than one copy, I have chosen whichever seems to be the most authoritative. Where there are both autograph and copies, I have not felt it necessary to record variant readings. In almost every case, the texts are being made available for the first time, so it is important to give them exactly as they were written; except where there is clearly a simple error, therefore, I have reproduced the spelling and layout of the originals, even where this has led to inconsistencies. Many of the poems are dated and I have organised them as far as possible in chronological order, with the exception that, as in the volume of James Austen's poems, I have grouped the word games – verse charades, bouts-rimés and noun verses – together at the end.

The Neck of Veal*

Poor neck of Veal, dont pity me
For pity more belongs to thee,
Though I've not tasted of thy meat
I've had the pleasure of seeing my Father eat.

*these lines were the first I ever made, I *think* I was
not *above* six years old at the time.

To Papa with a Knife

Though superstitious folk may say,
That if a knife you give away*
T'will end the love of Friends most true
Yet I feel sure I ne'er shall rue
The Day I gave this Knife to you.

For I am certain that no steel
Can cut the love, which I shall feel
For ever, for my parent dear
Therefore my father do not fear
This little present to receive
And me your ever duteous Son beleive.

JEA.

To Mamma

My grateful thanks, my Mother dear,
Accept for each box in the Ear
   Which you have given to me.
I hope that I shall have as few
When I alas! away from you
   At Ramsbury* shall be.

The Patriot

1

Soon as was known in great Dean Town
    That Rioters so bold
In Warwick most audaciously
    Their Banners did unfold

2

The Patriot Smalbone* on his horse
    Did instantly appear
In his dear country's own good cause
    Despising every fear

3

Directly he spurred on amain
    With fury guile enflamed
And rode with such amazing Speed
    His Horse he almost lamed.

4

But sometimes terror will oertake
    The bravest & the best,
And in mid battle with this fear,
    Great Smalbone was oppress'd.

5

For when he heard the Cannons roar
    And men their muskets pop,
He wish'd he had been safe at home
    In his own baking shop.

6

At last in safety he return'd
His family to greet,
And lay the laurels he had won
At Mrs Liney's* feet

The Races

1

Theyve fixed on the place, for the new 'pointed race*
    Which drives half the country mad,
The workmen declare, they all will go there,
    Though their work's wanted ever so bad.

2

The Squire's pursuing, the high road to ruin
    By gambling racing & betting,
Of horses they've twenty, & jockey's in plenty
    And the turf only wants a good wetting

3

The rain comes with speed, many fine days succeed,
    The course will look wonderous gay
There are Booths in a row, which make a great show,
    To the race let us hasten away.

1811

Fox hunting commenced

1

Alas! Brother reynard the races are over
    This morning the hounds are to meet,
No longer to us any safety in cover
    Our only support are our feet

2

Ah! why for this rain did the Methodists pray
    That Folk might [not] go to the race?
Forgetting that same rain would open a way
    For a sin full as crying "The Chase"

3

Hark! surely I hear them along the steep lane
    The red coats will soon he all here.
Alas to us foxes, for thanks to the rain
    The scent will be famous* I fear

4

E'er evening dear friend one of us two must die
    For this I will sure take my oath
And if we neglect very swiftly to fly
    I fear we perhaps may have both.

13

On the Dummer Harriers

1

First rising at morn I enquire with care
  What sort of a night it has been
And with pleasure I hear the day's open & fair
  And the Frost is no more to be seen.

2

Then John* I exclaim, take care that by eight
  You bring round my hunter so fleet
I would not for worlds get one moment too late
  To the place where the harriers meet.

3

Arrived at the cover I happily find
  There in very good time I am got
And 5 minutes after on looking behind
  I see them come towards me full trot.

4

Scarce thrown into cover little bounty* we hear
  To open upon a fine trail
Then Comely & Tously, says Canning* no fear
  But they'll soon have her up without [fail]

5

Then hansomely, also the rest falling in,
  They trail'd her all up to her form
Then the shouts of hun[t]sman & sportsmen begin
  All through the wide cover to storm

6

To the woods utmost limits the hare swiftly flew
　　When he* heard all the hounds on the scent
When to me as I stood there I came out a view*
　　"Gone away" I did cry as she went.

7

O'er a fine open country the hare takes her course
　　And a fine blazing scent we have got
Full cry runs each hound, & fast gallops each horse
　　Pleased, pulling, & eagar & hot

8

O'er stubbles & grass Fields, the scent lying high
　　Collected, together they run,
Their noses upraised., see how swiftly they fly,
　　Oh! hunting is capital Fun.

9

On a sudden at length o'er a fallow the scent
　　Entirely fail'd every hound
Then Buxam & Tosspot their footstep each bent
　　In casting the fallow all round

10

Look there at old Duster, observe pray how he
　　Is hunting that hedgerow about
In there she's laid down,—there she runs dont you see,
　　I thought we should soon have her out

11

I see she's dead tired, I'm sure, by her pace,
    She cannot get out of their view;
And I'll wager my life, that since that is the case
    Five minutes her business will do

12

Observe the old hounds, how they now take the lead
    They know she is sinking full well
And soon by the mouth of the dogs she must bleed
    Where panting she lies in that dell

13

Poor pussey*, she hears all the Dogs coming nigh,
    And yet is unable to rise;
See, how swiftly the hounds all at once on her fly
    She shrieks, yields, & struggles & dies.

Dirt & slime

Well I remember, once Papa.
When going home to see Mamma
    From Kintbury* so gay;
Some very pretty verses* made
On every tree & hill & shade,
    He saw upon his way.

Through these the muses charmed he led
Who pleased as punch* well crown'd his head
    With never fading bays,
But though the self same way I rode
Unto the very same abode
    Far different are my lays.

For much he praised each noble tree
Each hillock, forrest, Down & lee
    And all such daysyish stuff,
But the tenacious dirt & slime
That keeps impression such a time,
    I neer can pralse enough.

But for that charming dirt & slime
I might have wander'd to some clime
    Far distant all alone
I might have ridden into Spain,
And never seen you all again,
    Or to cold Russia gone;

I might have been on Affric's sands,
Or fallen into Arrab's hands,
    Or in Siberia laid,

Have wander'd on the banks of Tweed,
Or in the Highlands, or indeed,
  Where might I not have stray'd,

For courteous reader, you must know,
E'er with my tale I farther go,
  That the preceding night
A man & horse had gone that way
Whose footsteps deep mark'd in the clay
  Were still exposed to sight.

Thus when a good & steady hound,
In a deep wood his game has found,
  The best of all the pack,
Depending on his tender nose,
Tracing its footsteps swift he goes,
  Yet close upon the track,

Thus I did also all the time
Depending on the dirt & slime,
  And thus I found my way
For had that road been made of stone,
Or filled with gravelly soil alone,
  I might have stray'd all day.

And so in my poor humble rhyme,
The usefulness of dirt & slime,
  I'll make all people feel;
For it conducted me safe home,
Nor longer suffer'd me to roam
  Although I ran the heel.*

Address to Buonaparte

Where are those Men? say Tyrant where
Are those brave troops so beauteous fair?
That Army stout, & gallant Band
Which six months since from Gallia's Land*
Led by thy desperate ruthless hand
Their bloody course resistless bent
To Russia's region's wild extent
On Scythia's plains* they all have bled
Their Dastard Leader back has fled
Come Muse in measured Verse relate
Their base defeat – deserved Fate
The hostile Army soon alarms
All Russia's bravest sons to arms
A hardy race both free and bold
Inured to Danger, Want & Cold –

The School-boys wish

Me impsh it omp a toimsbud
A gobredy a hoimsbud.
A glomp me aump bibredy
A Pounup toob a sibredy
An aump a bib a funshud
A Croismus oump a comesbud
Mub oump gaub a waysbud
Bub a maub oump staysbud
A Ramsburruddub* mibredy
Nauba agaund oump sibredy

To Anna, A riddle

Dear Anna look, & you will see
Beauty & grace combined in me;
But think not that all mortals share
The Sight of all this beauty rare
For it is only shew'n to you
And to some other chosen few
For should some poor misshapen Elf
Or e'en this writer's very self
Presume on me to look, & stare
As if to view my beauty rare,
Unwilling that their vulgar eye
My dedicated charms should spy
Instant lose all form & grace
And represent [a] hideous face

To Anna

Whilst I am toiling here in vain
Some Verses from my scanty brain
Upon a subject hard, to write
My Sister, with a heart so light
Returning from the busy Race*
(Forgetful of my harder case)
Is now preparing wth. due Care
The Dress which she intends to wear
When at the ball wth. joyful heart
She'll sport some fashion new & smart
Forgetful did I say? Oh! no
I'm sure it never will be so
There can I'm certain be no fear
She'll ere forget her Brother Dear

Ramsbury* Sept[r]. 1812

The flower
To Anna
on her birthday

Anna, this little flowret take
And wear it for your Edwards* sake,
Tis the last time that I may pay
This tribute to your natal day.
I may not wander forth again
Through hedgerow thick & pathless glen
To seek among the twining groves
The flowret that my Sister loves
Th'unconscious month* shall still come round
But where will Anna then be found?*
Perhaps where Cumbria's precincts rear
Her rugged summits bleak & drear,
Perhaps, but hold, enough for me
At Steventon she will not be*
But still will Aprils showers produce
Anemonies for vulgar use
April! inconstant fickle vain,
Now bright with beams, now dark with rain
Seems as from heaven twere sent to show
Mans still more varying life of woe,
But I will pray that it may not
Prove emblem of your future lot.
But if my prayers should useless be
To ward adversity from thee
Should heav'n whose councils none may know
Think fit to try thee here with woe
Should you lose all your little wealth,
And that still greater blessing health

Whilst I've a cottage oer my head*
And one dry crust of barley bread
A wellcome guest approach, nor fear
Aught but a hearty wellcome there.
[Then] could we amongst all our woes
Still find a momentry repose;
We'd sit & talk of Friends since dead
And former pleasures long since fled,
Think o'er our pleasing youthful play
With which we wiled the hours away
Nor dream'd of greater check to joy
Than rainy day & broken toy.
Perhaps remember too this hour
And sigh at thoughts of this sweet flower.*
Then love this little flowret take
And wear it for your Edwards sake.

J E Austen

Ode of Horace imitated

My Father, to whose constant care thy boy
Owes every blessing he does now enjoy,
My ready refuge in the time of need
My best adviser, and my Friend indeed.
Many there are who only take delight
To see the racer urge his rapid flight,
To Epsom Races take their annual course
And Risk their fortune on a favourite horse
That Man who seeks by legislative fame
As patriotic Pitt* as great a Name
Him too who fills his garners with the corn
To Albions coasts from distant regions born
And that man also, who remote from strife
Enjoys the quiet of a country life
You'ld neer persuade by offering all the gold
Which mighty Attalus* possest of old
That cunning merchant in pursuit of gain
With trembling heart he'd plough the watry main.
When mountain like the lofty billows rise
And lowering clouds obscure the stormy Skies
The frighten'd Merchant fill'd with just alarm
Praises the quiet of a country Farm,
But soon refils his shatterd wreck again,
Untaught to bear a life of moderate pain.
Nor few are they, who oft midst noise & wine
Their health & fortune dayly undermine
Thus wasting half the precious Time which heaven
For nobler purposes to Man has given
Many in martial Toils & war delight
The Soldiers glory, & the Matrons fright.

The Sportsman too forgetful of his home
His wife & children cares not w[h]ere he roam
If the sly fox has met his eagour sight
Which cross an open country takes his flight.
This Sport I love, but me as yet a boy
My books & serious studies must employ
And my pursuit my latin verse & prose
However badly dayly to compose
But if at Oxford* I should gain a prize
I to the summit of my hopes should rise

1813

To Miss J Austen

No words can express my dear Aunt my surprise
Or make you concieve how I open'd my Eyes,
Like a pig Butcher Pile* has just stuck with his knife
When I heard for the very first time in my life
That I had the honour to have a relation
Whose works were dispersed through the whole of the nation
I assure you however I'm terrably glad,
Oh dear, just to think, (& the thought drives me mad)
That dear Mrs Jennings's* good natured strain
Was really the produce of your witty brain,
That you made the Middletons, Dashwoods & all
And that you, (not young Ferrars,) found out that a ball
May be given in cottages* never so small
And though Mr Collins* so grateful for all
Will Lady de Burgh his dear patroness call
Tis to your ingenuity really he ow'd
His living, his wife, & his humble abode.
Now if you will take your poor nephews advice
Your works to Sir William,* pray send in a trice,
If he'll undertake to some grandees to show it,
By whose means at last the Prince regent might know it
For Im sure if he did in reward for your tale
He'd make you a countess at least without fail
And indeed if the Princess should lose her dear life,
You might have a good chance of becoming his wife.*

The Lion & the Fox
a Fable

When first the Fox the lion saw
Struck dumb with reverence & awe
    He sunk beneath his feet.
The second time he courage took,
Could even bear on him to look
    And do obeisance meet.

But when again sly reynard stood
Before the monarch of the wood,
    Up to him straight he walks.
No sign of reverence displays,
But eyes him with an equal gaze
    And impudently talks.

Tis thus the child of 3 years old
When by the nurse maid she is told
    That company's below,
Comes down obediant to command
While her stuff'd mouth contains her hand
    And down her head hangs low.

But when she's recond 4 more years
No more oppress'd by infant fears
    She romps about the room,
Saucy she pulls each guest about
And by he[r] noisy ceaseless rout
    She pesters all who come

On the death of L B Wither Esq[re].

My dearest Friend you bid me write*
And sure your wish I cannot slight
Although the thing which now you ask
Will be to me no easy Task
But if I try to do my best
I trust you'll pardon all the rest.
Your conduct in this dire distress
Prove you a feeling heart posses
And I am very proud, tis true,
Of having such a friend as you.
Yet dearest William check your grief
Let reason bring her sure relief
Tis sad indeed to see a Friend
Or loved relation slowly bend
Worn by degrees towards his End
But must lessend [sic] much the woe
Of this sad scene this dredful blow
To know for certainty, as you
My dearest Friend must surely do
That he whom you do now lament
Was well prepared eer he went
To quit this scene of Griefs & Woes
And the poor pleasures it bestows
Whose exemplary life on Earth
Had prov'd to every one his worth
An upright Judge of honest Mind
A neighbour good, a Father kind
And in whose placid brow serene
Domestic virtues might be seen,
And now, from worldly Cares removed,
By all lamented & beloved,
Deservedly in heaven obtains

The due reward of all his pains:
Though now no more the rolling year
Restores you to your Gransire dear
Nor when the holy-days are come
Shall you again returning home
Behold once more his reverend Face
And share with Joy his warm Embrace,
Yet think not that forever you
Will be excluded from his view:
For well remember, Mans whole Life
Resembles School* in care & strife:
In both we're station'd to become
More worthy of out future home
And as at School the hardships there
Which we are always forced to bear
Makes us enjoy so much the more
The pleasures Home contains in store
And as the more the Youth may fag
And never at his learning lag
By so much more through life he gains
The due reward of all his pains;
Thus in proportion as the Man
Does in this world the best he can
Will God (from whom all bounties flow) *
Greater rewards on him bestow.
And when your course of life is run
And all your earthly labours done
And when this fleeting life you leave
You'll your reward in Heav'n receive,
There in a state of bliss compleat
Again your grandsire you will meet
And there of happiness secure
You'll fear nor death nor Sorrow more.

April 1813

To Manydown

Sweet Manydown,* thou scene of Pleasures past,
Ah why do days of pleasure fly so fast!
Receive the Tribute of this humble lay,
From one who owe[s], what he can ne'er repay
Full many a[n] hour of Mirth, & many an hour of play
How much I love in ev'ry well known place
Pleasing remembrance of the past to trace,
In lifes long days whateer my lot may be
My thoughts shall rest with pleasure upon thee
Thou in my heart an interest wilt posses,
Which Time may strengthen but can not make less
Een thy defects are pleasing, for they all
Back to my mind some past Events recal
The Ha! ha! often clear'd in Sportive bound,
The tall green gates which tower above the ground
The garden where I often loved to stray
When partial gleams adornd bright Aprils day
And see upon the fostering wall appear
The forward blossoms of the early year,
Or mark the pease* in beautiful array
Their breard* white leaves & fragrant blooms display
When scarce in other gardens more exposed
The bursting mould the latent shoot disclosed
These were thy real comforts, when thy late
And rev^d. master* own[ed] thy wide Estate,
He rest[s] in Heav'n & he who fills his place*
Would all these beauties for a sweep deface,
Green gates, & ha! ha!, garden, walls, & all
In one oerwhelming common ruin fall.
But thou the scene of all my former plays

Where with my friend I spent my infant days
Such alteration. needs must undergo
That friend himself shall no such changes know
And may [I] in my William ever find
A noble, generous, & well grown mind,
True to his friends affectionate & kind.

December 29 1813

To Miss C. Craven

Hard is the task which you have laid
Upon your Cousin lovely maid
Yet Ladies suit like Minstrels strain
By man must neer he heard in vain
So that I fear I cant refuse
To raise my long neglected Muse.
I find it hard, but do not deem
The fault existing in my theme,
For dull must be that Poets Lyre
Which even beauty cant inspire
Yet you must own tis hard for me
To sing of mirth & revelry,
For me immured within these walls*
Which Echo but to noise & brawlls
Whose hours are spent in pooring o'er
Volumes antique of ancient lore
Hard must it be for such to tell
The envy of each rival belle
To paint the wondering gaze of all
When first you figured at a ball
Such subjects far for me too hard
I leave for some more able bard
While I to sing your praises try
By classical mithology.

Cupid, 'tis said, one Summer's day
Threw in a pet his darts away,
While rising tears full well confest
The sorrows of his little breast.
"Alas how times are changed," he said,

33

"Since first I [ply'd] my lawless trade
Time was, when Beauty join'd to love
Could triumph over man or Jove
But now alas my reign is past
And Lucre rules the world at last.
Men are such mercenary Creatures
They care not, they, for form in features
My darts are useless now I'm told
Unless I dip their points in Gold
And hearts are now so hard & light
Tis past my art to wound them quite.
These words he utterd with a sigh
Which reached his Mothers ears on high,
"To me" she answerd "it belongs,
My Cupid, to redress your wrongs
I will produce a human creature
So exquisite in form & feature
That men so obdurate before
Perforce shall see her & adore
Through her you shall triumphant reign
Come take your quiver once again."
She said, & quicker than the thought
The Sister graces quickly sought
Their joint assistances to entreat
This perfect figure to compleat
Nor begged in vain, each different grace
Adorn'd the figure, form, & face
Apollo gave his Lyre, & skill
To wake its soothing notes at will,
And Education too combined
With these the virtue* of the mind.
Thus formed for conquest, thus inspired,

34

E'en Venus saw her & admired,
Then sent her image down from heaven
And smiled, & called her "Charlotte Craven".

My story's ended, but I hear
My Muse is whispering in my ear
The World will say, I'm not sincere
And many will affirm that I
Have dipp'd my pen in flattery.
Let them, I care not if they do,
For I can prove my words are true,
Tell them my muse to go to Speen
And mark her figure, air & mien,
How fine her form, her face how fair,
And call it flattery if they dare.

September 1814

To Mrs B. Lefroy. On her Wedding day

November's blasts are rough & rude,
    November's frosts are sharp & chill,
And yet, despite thy sternest Mood,
    November, I will love thee still.

Thou first beheldst me breathing here,*
    I date my increasing age from thee,
And still returning year by year
    Thou prov'st a Month of Joy to me.

And now tis thine, sweet Month, tis thine
    My Anna's Marriage rites to view,
To *see* her former Joys resign
    And bid us all a long Adieu;

To see her seek, nor seek in vain
    If ought avail my earnest prayer,
Securer pleasures free from pain,
    Unpinch'd by want, unworn by care.

Then fated morn auspicious rise,
    And cheer us with thy brighter ray,
Forget Novembers stormy Skies,
    And smile like April, for a day;

Or if a few light drops the while
    Should falling Dim thy brighter Shine,
Disperse them gently with a smile
    And let our Morn & Eve be fine.

A tear is due to pleasures past –
     A tear to parting friends is due,
But let not the impression last
     Let brighter prospects close the view.

***

Tis done, tis oer, & oh may She
     This day of Joy with joy remember,
And even have a cause like me
     To speak with pleasure on November.

Winchester Nov. 1814

A Letter to Miss Caroline Austen
Winchester. Saturday night*

Yes lady to his promise just,
Your brother has discharged his trust,
Yes yes this poor unvaliant Knight
This poor Red Button.* whom you sleight,
Has kept his word, & sends with speed
This letter which you now shall read,
Nay more, you'll see the truth I speak
It shall not hold one word of Greek
Nor will I give a line to tell
What to Demosthenes* befell,
And so papa will never know
Whether we read him yet or no.
Beside my dearest girl I ween
I've better than my promise been
For, unless bad my memory grows
I only promised some in prose
So now no more can be your due,
For one in rhyme must go for two.
Yes it is true, but I hope though
This truth all people will not know,
Or else good Mr Croft* may say
That you as if for two should pay.
Which thing (as now go on the times)
You'd think was paying dear for rhymes.
Now if I do not pass my bounds
By venturing to mention hounds
I wish that you papa'd desire
As you sit round the parlour fire
When next they meet at Ashengrove*

To give my love to poor Truelove.*
Now lest you think I only write
To give you present, short delight
I'll now explain a little plan
As plainly as a poet can.
That when you've puzzied oer my letter
And thought how you'd have made a better
You'd set my lines to music sharp
Upon your curious new made Harp,*
Then sing it to the pigs & sow
The Horses Donkey & the Cow.*
And honour your unworthy Bard
By making them dance round the yard.
With best love to papa, mamma
Dora & Lady Julia*
Would such a lofty Lady deign
To listen to my humble strain
I must conclude my note & be
Your most obedient JE.
PS. You must remember I am sure
When playing on the parlour floor
You often challenged me to fight
For which I owe you still a spite
So now I *challenge* you to write

    I challenge thee this very night
       To try your rival muse
     And if you are a stainless Knight
      I'm sure you cant refuse.

On Westminster Abbey

Yes thou art Grandieurs self thou Nature's boast*
Thou most respected where thour't injurd most
By times rough hand, which adds a nameless grace
Een to the very Image it deface.
Where we can turn from Bacons modern stone*
Where every muscle as in life is shown
Whose every passion of the Feature plays
We might suppose its guest in former days
And gaze with wondering reverential awe
On Block ill fashioned without form or law
Where sleeps some Hero none ee'r heard or saw
Is it the Sombre brown which times long night
Has cast oer what though shapeless once was white?
Is it the time worn line which half a day
Can scarce decipher, & can only say
That once the doughty Knight Sir Barnard* led
A band of Warriors, & he now is dead?
That thus can facinate the mind to gaze
For their years sake on works of former days
No! – tis a feeling of the nobler mind
Which, felt by all, can be by few defined
A feeling wild romantic & sublime
Raised wilder by obscurity & time,
The gazers busy fancy can conceive
Till forced her own vagaries to beleive
His exploits, virtues, weaknesses & Pride
Of whom we only know he lived & Died
Fancy with colors rather high than true
Most pleased to act where most remains to do
So sadly stinted in her flight, in sooth

In newer structures by the voice of truth.
Where to some modern Lord the Bustos* rise
Or the carved stone tells where the Statesman lies
Too* faithful memory of more recent days
Will often contradict the Sculptured praise
We can remember well his every crime
Unsoftend by oblivion and time
And while we feel their consequences yet
It is too soon to pardon & forget.
& must truth always thus cramp fancys flight
& thus bring failings mixt with good to light?
No while we gaze upon the Bust of Pitt*
& think of Goodness Eloquence and Wit
Of pure & Patriot rectitude – Can ought?
Of blame or censure once possess a thought?
Blest be the Art that can thus nobly raise
The grateful tribute of a Nations Praise.
Oh could my lines with feelings full as warm
Catch half the spirit of that Sculptured form
Where Anarchy with wild & furious Air
Shakes his strong Chain & rages in Despair
And history sits securely by his side
& writes his efforts with complaisant pride
This is a Nations gift,* & worthy tis
Such pledge be given by such Isle as this
To prove to every other Foreign Land
Brittons are grateful for a saving Hand
Oh could we quit this Pile with such a thought
We then might think our Country all it ought,
But we must pass through Londons greedy* street
& scenes of Riot & intemperence meet
Must see a Rable selfish wild & rude

Who *seem* at least incapable of good
So little here seems right so much amiss
We soon are forced to ask our reason this
Are *these* the Men the Patriot toiled to Save?
Are *these* the Men who thus adorn his grave

Feb:– 1815

The Wood walk* ... To Anna

And art thou come once more to see a Spot
Which seems by all now thou art gone forgot?
And art thou come to view each well known Scene
And think of what is now & what has been?
But will it give the most of joy or pain
To tread each former footstep o'er again?
Or canst thou leave without one silent Tear
A place so loved through many a recent year?
For thou didst love it, aye, & lov'dst it well
For its own sake as many proof can tell
There would'st thou stray when low beneath the west
The Sun has set & left the world to rest
When the still leafe scarce felt the sinking breeze
And Evening's shades clos'd in in slow degrees
And thou mights[t] start from some aerial dream
Roused by the roosting Peacock's distant scream
And later yet, when every breeze was still
Nor stird the leafe nor screamd the Peacock shrill
Still would'st thou stray, nor feel in such a scene
The dew drops rising on the spangled green
Nor yet alone when Summer Charms were spread
But een when winter rear'd her rugged head
When every object that could meet the sight
Was one unvaried Mass of glaring white
Still would'st thou go, in this belov'd retreat
Alike were winter's Colds & Summer's Heat.
But now in this neglected path the snow
May come unnoticed, & unnoticed go,
Nor can a footstep or a trace be found
To break the sameness of the flake strewn ground

Save where the robins slender prints declare
That he has sought a kindly shelter there
And would have sung, hadst thou been there to hear
And pay with crumbs the strains which pleas'd thy Ear
Or where thy brothers fond tho' careless feet
Have sought the place becaus[e] twas thy retreat,
But he's away, & who does now remain
To seek a walk which gives such pleasing pain
Or love a spot however sweet & fair
The more because thou loved'st to wander there.
But he shall come, & here shall love to lie
While Summer gales shall sing his lullaby
And there shall dream with thee he seeks this walk
With thee to ramble, & with thee to talk
In one vain hour, if what can please be vain,
Live all his years of Childhood oer again;*
Untill some envious gnat his sleep shall break
And all his visions fly him as he wake
And he shall start & own that it does seem
That human happiness is but a dream.*

March 1815
Winchester

To Caroline on her birthday

Nine are gone, the tenth appears,
And June again her blossoms rears,
Again her clear & piercing ray
Penetrates the leafy spray
Through our church walks mazes winding
Annually fresh beauties finding,
Since it first began to shine
On my darling Caroline.
Lovely as the loveliest flower
Wash'd by April's freshest shower,
But, although far firmer made
Liable, like that to fade
Though in ev'ry roseate streak
Health seems painted in thy Cheek,
Yet this May has proved too true
Sickness e'en may visit you.
Though the pitying hand of Heaven
Back to life my darling's given
For unlike the flower that dies
That another may arise,
Had'st thou fall'n beneath the stroke,
Were thy frame by sickness broke
When had June returned to view
One as loved, as dear as you?
No, clear shining oft again,
It had look'd & sought in vain
One with like esteem & grace
Filling thy regretted place,
But in each remembering breast
Then thy Image deep imprest;

While with sorrowful concern
All had seen thy Month return.
Tis not so; the tenth is come
But to see returning bloom
In you, as it used to see
Full of Spirits, life & glee
Loved by Father, Sister, Mother,
And, though last not least, by Brother.
Then may each revolving year
Mark fresh graces still appear.
Never may it cease to find
All the father in thy mind,
All the Mothers graces mild,*
Centerd in the favourate child.

On the defeat of Buonaparte at Waterloo

Hark, from each sacred Turret's ivied Tower
What grateful peals of heartfelt Triumph pour?
Joy reigns through all, each gloomy face is clear'd
Of those who doubted, & of those who fear'd.
Yet fear who may while Wellington remain,
And British forces follow to the Plain.
He came, the once proud Tyrant of the world,
He came again from Empire to be hurl'd
Reckless what fate awaited those he led,
He met a Wellington, he fought & fled.
Ah alterd, fallen Gallia,* where is flown
That loyal Pride which once thou call'dst thy own?
Thou who wast once neath Bourbons just command*
The second Empire in Europas land
Whose praise was second on the voice of Fame,
Nor knewst to tremble but at Albions* Name
And could'st thou then thy anxious King forsake*
And chuse a Tyrant for a Tyrants sake?
See'st thou not now in thy approaching fate
And mourn'st thou not thy Error all too late?
Again mid battle's broils thy Leader fled
And still fresh honors heaped on Welsley's Head.*
Albion, exult in thy encreasing fame,—
And Britons glory in a Britons Name!
But ah, why, mixt with ev'ry pealing bell,
Thus slowly sounds the sad & solemn knell?
Why oer the Pages which these Tidings bear
Does yonder Parent drop that fervent Tear?
Ask Ye the cause? That dreadful Column read
Which tells how many for their country bleed

How many a hopeful youth in early death
Sighs for his country with his latest breath
And these thy works, thou Tyrant. On thy head
Shall all this misery be at length repaid,
For justice due the fathers voice shall cry,
And thou shalt tremble at the widows sigh,
When he the last the latest judge of all
For ev'ry added crime shall doom a deeper fall!!

Winchester July 1815

The Heroes

I ask not the aid of Parnassus's quire*
    I call not on Helicon's stream,
Small need of their presence the bard to inspire
What dunce would not feel a poetical fire,
    When a Hero & conquest's his theme.

Ye Sea Nymphs & Nayids,* who watch oer the seas,
    Which circle round Albion's coast,
Spread mild oer the ocean, your gentlest breeze
And waft to our country, in safety & ease,
    All Europe's, Pride, Honour, & Boast.

Full long has old England been justly renown'd
    (May that National virtue ne'er cease,
As fair hospitality's favourite ground,
But how can a worthy reception be found
    To hail the restorers of peace.

Oh hush, for a welcome allready I hear,
    Full worthy of each honour'd guest,
The thanks of a country, victorious, sincere,
And what than such thanks, can we fancy more dear
    To a patriot warriors breast,

Brave Blucher,* thou veteran, gallant though gray,
    I could titles & riches reject,
With thee to change places for one fleeting day,
To]ook round upon Europe thus peaceful & say
    All this, I have help'd to effect.

Epitaph on old Justice

Here lies than whom a better hound
Might neer o'er hill or vally bound
    To chase the caitiff Fox.
Whose foot was fleet & nose was good
Throu fallow field or dripping wood
    Or scent destroying box

But all these virtues could not save
Poor Justice from a bloody grave
    The cruel cord is bound
This wimper reaches Georges ear,
But pity is a stranger there
    He hangs the veteran hound.

But ah! admit not oh my muse
The hardy huntsmans stern excuse
    For this his cruelty
For he would say his Eyes were dim
That age had loosen'd every limb,
    In short he was to die.

Can you no cause more proper give
Why this poor hound must cease to live
    No juster reason find?
For loss of eye his life must end!
Do you not know my worthy friend
    That justice should be blind

Soon shall your kennel as I wene
Appear a wild & lawless scene
     Of rapine & disarray
Plunder shall now securely stalk
And *Gamester* all unpunish'd walk
     For *Justice* is away.

Een *Liberty* her head shall hide,
No more her cast* so free & wide
     The puzzled pack will aid
And then will *Blucher** deign to grace
So lawless & defiled a place
     Whence *Liberty* has stray'd?

Will glory wait the conqueror now?
Will Laurel twine above his brow?
     Oh no! it cannot be
For when we hear the passing Bell
For upright justice, then farewell
     Glory & Liberty.

Ulisses announces to Hecuba that the Manes*
of Achilles demand the death of Polixena

Yes still the same, though Priams Towers fall
Though royal slaughter stain the sacred wall,
Though reft of Crown, of Country, Sons, & Lord,
A wretched captive to a Foe abhorred,
That Air of Majesty, that stately Mein,*
To all around her still proclaim the Queen.
Unhappy Hecuba, of all these bereft,
Yet hast thou still one darling comfort left,
For fair as Helens self, & good as fair,
One daughter sooths a captive Mother's Care,
Still mayst [thou] weep with her oer former pain,
And live a life of suffering oer again,
Still may she sorrowing at a Brothers Toomb

To Mamma.

And have I written since the earliest ray
Of infant reason could afford a Lay,
And have I found, as it almost would seem,
In evry subject, except one, a theme?

Moses

*Written at Winchester by J.E. Austen. In Commoners**

"Moses, stand forth! confess thy power now vain;
Nor dupe a Nation with thy words again.
Moses stand forth! attend to Israel's cry,
Nor stand inactive while thy people die.
Cause as thou art of evils yet endured,
Thy threats compelled us, or thy arts allured;
Changing the Labourers for the starveling's sigh,
We fled from bondage – but we fled to die.
With fruitless care we slew our paschal lamb,*
And scaped the plagues that swept the land of Ham.*
The land of Ham has many a pleasant spring,
Safe from the fury of the Heavenly King.*
Wide o'er her plains, the king of waters flows,
The gourd swells luscious, & the fig tree blows.
While we, the Lord's, by various evils curs't
Find not a spring to slake our burning thirst.
Where, where's the boasted justice of his Throne,
To feed the alien, & neglect his own?
Moses stand forth! attend to Israel's cry,
Nor stand inactive while thy people die – "
With rising clamour, & increasing din,
Thus Israel murmured* in the plains of Sin.*
Fierce from the drought, their high impatient soul
Spurned at obedience, & defied control –
Poured out reproaches on their Friend & Guide,
Provoked their mightier God,* & half his power denied.
Stand forth! they cried while half in art to cast,
They eyed each stone* which glittered as they past –

And muttering threats & curses as they went,
Approached their venerable leader's tent.
Stand forth! they cried – Yet when the Senior came
The loudest murmurer felt a transient shame –
Firm was his step, serenely calm his air
For conscious innocence & truth were there –
As bursts refulgent* from the clouds unfurled
The sun breaks forth upon the stormy world,
Bids the loud wind & louder thunder cease,
And lulls the troubled elements to peace
So Moses bade the clarmorous murmurs break;
And silence settled as the Father spake –
"Ungrateful minions!* can ye thus forget
The hand which saved you, & sustains you yet?
Showed your dread passage through the opening deep*
And sunk your Foemen at one desperate sweep?
Raise murmurers, raise your eyes, before your camp
By day your guider, & by night your lamp,
See ye the pillar of the Lord* appear,
And dare to doubt the hand which placed it there.
Did you not hunger, & receive your fill?
Think on the streams of Marah,* & be still! –
Look on yon plain – behold the sandy wild
On which no wheat has waved – no culture smiled
But seems, exulting in its barren soil
To mock the ploughshare, & to laugh at toil.
Yet from these wilds, the sun's meridian height –
Has scarcely swept the Manna* from your sight –
Look at yon rock! no cavity contains
The niggard savings of the partial rains;
Or if it does – the fowls of Heaven have quaffed
The scarce fall'n moisture for their scanty draught.

But there the Lord his mercies shall proclaim
And Horeb's rock shall speak his people's shame."
He spake, & pointed – in his listener's eyes
He read distrust, displeasure & surprise –
Yet still, that voice accustomed to obey,
The murmurers followed, as he led the way.
In naked boldness, on the level wild
By nature's hand irregularly piled
Arose the rock – its tops no blade supplied
No lichens hung around it's naked side –
Supremely barren, in a barren plain,
It lacked the seal of desolation's reign.
In such a scene have fabling Poets said
Prometheus* suffered, while the Vultures fed.
O'er the bare space, the wildest winds that blow
Raise but the sands, from the expanse below.
The sunbeam striking on the rugged pile
Show'd it more black, more ghastly in it's smile –
There Moses stood;* around, the wondering band
Watched each slow motion of his lifted hand.
Back on his neck his streaming locks were driven,
Fixed was his ardent eye – & fixed on Heaven!
His left hand grasped his simple robe – his right
Stretched to the rock his wand of potent might –
"Thou God of Israel, hear thy people's cry –
Forgive their murmurings, & their wants supply.
This rod has struck the proud Egyptian's head,
The seas have felt it, & the winds obeyed!
Thou Lord of Israel, guide thy servant's hand,
The rock shall open, at it's Lord's command!"
He struck – the rock beneath the potent rod,
Shook to it's centre, & confessed it's God;

While gushing waters from it's opening side
Proclaimed that power, the impious crowd denied –
The thirsty soil & sand receding gave
An ample channel for the rushing wave.
Far, far it flowed along the yielding mould;
Exulting nature gladdened* as it rolled,
Wild from his Lord the conscious camel burst,
The kid & lion rushed to quench their thirst:
It's gladdened banks spontaneous flowerets bore;
And Israel murmured at their God no more!

Jan^y, 1816

To the Memory of Miss Jane Austen,
who was buried in the North Aisle of Winchester Cathedral

In Venta's consecrated Pile,*
　　Where every swelling note,
Streams softly down the central Aisle,
　　Oer hallow'd graves to float,

Where Fancy mourns reclined in death
　　The Warton whom she loved,*
And stately Wyckham* sleeps beneath
　　The Column he improved,

Low in that Awe-inspiring Seat,
　　Thou fair, lamented Maid,
Where Piety and Genius meet,
　　Right justly wert thou laid.*

If purest Taste, if brightest Mind,*
　　If humblest Piety,
Alone mid such a rest mind find;
　　Who had excluded thee?

The purple Flowret of the Vale,*
　　Around its perfume throws,
But, though it scent the evening Gale,
　　We know not when it grows.

E'en so, thy Volumes to the world
　　Have half thy merit spread,
Yet were those graces yet unfurl'd
　　The Eye alone could read.

And who of all the Tribe, to whom
    Thy works amusement gave,
Have felt one sorrow for thy doom,
    Or know thy early grave?

Yet on thy birth no sickly ray
    From brilliant Genius fell;
Yet Nature hail'd thy Natal Day,
    Who sketch'd her form so well.

Man's lighter Follies saw their Doom,
    And own'd their Tyrant born;
While Satire sprung from Cowper's Tomb*
    But woke without his Horn.*

Teeming with mimic Life was found
    Each Offspring of thy Quill:
Though fell the Scene on Fiction's ground,
    Twas Nature's Shadow still.

In humble Life's untrodden Vale
    Twas thy delight to stray;
For there were flowers to grace thy Tale,
    And weeds to lop away.

And well may they, thou pleased'st so much,
    Thy early loss deplore –
That magic Wand has ceased to touch,
    Their feast of Wit is oer.

But we, to whom, unbidden Guests
 That feast was always spread;
In private who enjoy'd thy Jests,
 And in thy presence fed;

We, who the closest kindred claimed
 With one so doubly dear, –
From us may fall, perchance unblamed,
 One half-repining Tear.*

Who, till they *saw* the youthful hue,
 The Sunshine of that face,
That Mirror true, in which we view,
 The minds reflected grace,

Could think twice twenty winters past,
 In this dark Vale of Woe,
So mild, so soft a Shade could cast,
 Their silent lapse to show?

For till unvaried, genial, warm,
 Each Season pass away;
Till dark November breeds no storm,
 Nor bids a Flower decay;

Each circling year, must see the tear
 Of human Sorrow fall,
Still Grief & Care the Cheek must wear,
 And they are doom'd to all.

Perchance tis selfish Tears alone
    That leave the lasting Stain,
And thou had'st left unwept thy own,
    To mourn anothers pain.

And Grief & Care, my Cheek may wear,
    And Sorrow mark each Year;
It can but serve my heart to tear,
    From all that binds me here.

But oh! however doom'd to grieve,
    Whateer my losses be,
Still let twice twenty Winters leave
    A Mind as pure to me;

For sure, if Soul its part c^d. play
    Upon this vice staind scene,
Nor bear one transient spot away,
    Unspotted thine had been –

No, though unsullied leaves the Snow
    The cloud that gave it birth,
It shall not pass one hour below
    Without some stain of Earth –

And een to thee, great change shall be,*
    To make thee quite divine,
The blood that saved a Magdalen's Soul*
    Was shed alike for thine.

J.E. Austen
Sunday September 28th: 1817.

Letter to Mrs. B. Lefroy. Wyards*
After a Basingstoke Ball*

To your letter, dear Anna, though hard-pressed for time,
I'm attempting to send you an answer in rhyme,
My dress & my partners to paint to your Eye,
And in Heraldry Terms to your questions reply.
And first for myself, now of course you'll be sure,
My visage was *proper*, my buttons were orr,
My Trowsers were sable, & azure my coat,
And argent the neckcloath surrounding my Throat.
My figure was rampant, at least while poussetting,
But couchant became, while the tea things were getting.
I, by two cups of Tea, kept my senses from slumber,
But I know not their hue, though I do know their number.
Wether *sable* or *vert*,* [1] M^rs. Blackstone* can best tell
But the Sugar and Cream were as white as a Vestal.
My Manners were such, as I cannot describe,
And I danced – like the Chief of a Cannibal Tribe;
The Ladies I honoured by chusing, you'll see,
Are all good in their way, – tho' not equal to me;
With Miss Standen I never am likely to dance,
T'would delight her, no doubt, but she has not a chance;
My Labours began with Miss Caroline Wiggett;*
Then with Margaret Blackstone* my luck was to jig it,
Miss [2] Chambers, a damsel of gentle degree,
Happy Girl, was the next to stand opposite me:
After that you might see me, my heart greatly hurting,
With a sweet M^rs. Oxenham, just come to Worting
Then, to prove I possest too much bottom to tire
I the Boulanger danced with the charming [3]Maria.
And so stately my Form, & so lovely her face,

Ne'er did Basingstoke Ball such a Boulanger* grace;
In fact, though the Chaperons declared twas so thin,
That with Ease Mr. Lane* co^d. contrive to get in;
Yet such was the charm I diffused through the train,
None who danced in my set, co^d. find cause to complain.

(1) M^rs. Blackstone made Tea.
(2) Miss Chambers to whom M^r. Augustus Hare* introduced
    me, was staying with Lady Jones.
(3) Maria Hasker, of course.

To the Memory of the Revd James Austen

Here, mid the Flock his fond attention fed,
A Village Pastor rests his reverend head.
Long had he felt affliction's chastening rod;
Long, marked for death, the paths of life he trod.
For talents honourd, though to few display'd,
And virtues brightening through dejection's shade,
Mildest of Men, his gentle Course he ran;
And lived & died, beloved of God, and Man.

Best, earliest Friend! thy sweet career is oer;
Thy kindness glads, thy Sorrows grieve no more.
Then heave *we* o'er thy tomb no mournful sighs;
Nor dream of sorrow where a Christian lies:
In one glad thought our selfish Murmurs cease –
The Lord hath let his Servant part in peace –*

64

Lines to Dyce written 1821

Ω Δυχε, –– ω φιλολογε ––*
  Thy wonder sure must rest
That Quintus Calaber* sh^d. be
  The brute I most detest.

2

Poor Quintus little thought, I ween,
  Of plans by him undone,
In the distant year of our Lord, eighteen
  Hundred & twenty one.

3

But who the ills can calculate
  A barbarous Austen pours,
A flood of ills which mocks at fate,
Which time nor space can terminate,
Which flows to times remotest date,
  To earth's remotest shores.

4

First, marring Childhoods pleasures, comes
  The joy destroying flood,
Midst boughs of birchen,* where many an Urchin
  Is doomed to shed his blood.

5

Onward, midst fields of toil & pain
  The bitter stream we meet,
Far from young health's athletic plain
  And pleasures green retreat.

Pale headache stalks its banks along,
    Where never laurel grew;
Thither the fool & pedant throng,
And e'en some generous sons of song,*
Drawn thither by attraction strong,
    Join the misguided crew.

A letter from an Undergraduate to his Friend, descriptive of the late Commemoration

My Lectures o'er, my Books packd up,
With naught to do, but dine & sup
    E'er Oxford's bade Adieu,
None disengaged with whom to talk,
Too light to sleep too hot to walk   5
    I'll wast* an hour with you –
To you the wondrous Tale to tell
Of Beauty's Flower in Learnings Cell,
While poor old Oxford scarcely knows
Whether she stands on head or Toes,   10
Full of such noise, such Balls,* such Belles,
Such Landauletts & Curricles.*
Yet do not think my Muse shall shine
Fetter'd to an heroic Line;
Too hot the day for her to march   15
With measured tread as stiff as starch
Like Conqueror through triumphal Arch,
Not standing upon Helicon*
    The Eye in a fine Phrensy roiling,*
But languid from this burning Sun   20
    Through Magdalens shadowy Elm trees strolling;
In Strain unlabourd, as she'd chuse
While chatting with each Sister Muse
And sipping for her Evening Tea
Cups of Nectareous Bohea*   25
While Water from Castalia* ta'en,
    Boil'd on an Altar, bubble,
Raised by some youth their smile to gain
Wh.om, just like me, a scribbler vain,

They laugh at for his Trouble.   30
A prettier Picture ne'er you'll see
Of the nine Muses drinking Tea.

But now for Oxford, know you not
The usual quiet of that Spot,
How pious founders raised each College   35
Sacred to dulness, wine, & Knowledge
Where Logic Euclid Aristotle
Meet oer the Common rooms full bottle,
While genius there so long retains
Her leading Strings,* they grow to chains   40
Where useless Learning, heartless Mirth abound,
And sacred Woman's a forbidden Sound –

   Yet know our grand Commemoration
Has summoned to us half the Nation
You see Barouch Landaus* & four   45
Stop at a Provost's Gothic door*
That Provosts self, with neater dress,
Meeting some family Lioness,
Learns, setting habit at defiance,
That most unacademic Science,   50
In which he never took degrees,
That very useless art – to please.
While others, hopeless to succeed
   In looking soft or civil
Wish the whole female prying breed   55
   At home – or at the Devil
As Pluto* shudderd with afright
For fear the Sun should visit
His cheerless realms, & bring to light

That scene, which shewn* much best in night   60
   For all the world to quiz it.

Yet so it is, young Ladies here
As thick as Gownsmen* now appear.
See how, while College friends with them mix,
Their Brothers look in Academics –*   65
Gaze upon Tufts* with reverence due –
On silk gowns* smile complacent too –
On Commoners* will waste a glance,
If their Coats look just come from France –
Of Servitors* enquire with doubt   70
If its a gownsman or a Scout*
(Tis strange how soon young Ladies learn
What Men to seek – & what to spurn)
See Parker's Prints,* & then are wild
For all on Spier's* Counter piled –   75
A Pincoushin,* a Woodstock glove,*
And fall in debt – or fall in love –

   Now to the Theatre,* for there
On Wednesday Morning all repair,
And ne'er at Drury* might you stare   80
On Peagantry more passing rare
   Or gaudier Dresses see –
And people say, I ween not true,
Their Parts are personated too,
The Doctors look so grave to view,   85
   Their Air of Sanctity –
I pass all that. I do not know
Though scarlet* oer their shoulders flow,
But that their Minds are white as Snow –

The outside of the platter's clean,*   90
And thats sufficient to be seen.
    But mark the long procession –
First Beadles* 8 with mace in hand
File on each side & take their stand,
    Right proud of their profession –   95
Next comes that mighty Man,* whose power
Blooms through 3 years, like Augusts flower
    The everlasting Pea –
Then pair by pair, in graceful fold
Of richest purple streakd with gold   100
    Move the Nobility –
Next march the Doctors, clad as red
As Butcher's Stalls where Steers have bled –
Stout Pillars they of Church & State,
Men, if not of worth, of weight, –   105
    Last bring up the rear –
Velvet their sleeve, & stout their stride,
Terror of Gownsmen far & wide
In annual magisterial pride
    The Proctors* twain appear.   110
Then Claps, like Thunder sent by Jove
Are heard propitious from above
As up the steps the pageants move
    And seat them silent down.
Slow doffs his Cap, that Man of might,   115
Some speech in Latin to recite,
Though none can catch his accents quite,
    Then readjusts his gown,
And flanked on each side by a Proctor
Makes many an honourary Doctor.   120
While thus the silent Conclave's seated,

E'er yet the Prises are repeated,
While Benefactors,* long since rotten,
Whose Tombs are broke, & worth forgotten,
Called from their rest in annual Oration,   125
Puzzle with names uncouth the convocation,
(Though worthier office well might fill
The Classic Bard of* [   ] Hill)

Since no one listens, let us too
　　On the Assembly pry   130
Confined, but variegated view,
　　Well worth attentive Eye;
Where rich Pellesse,* Bonnet wide,
And Spencer* puffd, serve but to hide
That form which each might shew with pride,   135
With rapture each behold,
As Gothic Taste w^d. overcrust
The pure grace of the marble Bust
　　With Coat of gaudy Gold.
But most I hate, oh shame upon it!   140
Yon shading tantalising Bonnet,
　　Where in perspective thrown,
Like Screen beyond the lengthend Aisle
Where we but see a [gorgeous] Pile
Of Beauty, all confused the while,   145
　　Though finely wrought the Stone,
Shews each fair Face, a Mass of Charms,
Which distance of its power disarms.
Yet not unbrilliant seems, or mean
Of silks & lace the chequered scene
　　Uprising, row on row.
As grottoes concave roofs appear

Of close set shells, a little sphere
Inverted in the mirror clear
　　Of streams that pass below.

Hark they begin! but why tell you
Who, all some tedious hours through.
　　Unheeded words rehearse.
The only thing that's listened to
　　Will be the English verse –
That youthful Poet proudly stands,
　　And decks the rostrum well –
And plaudits long, from Gownsmen's hands
　　Their loud approval tell.
More by his beauty than his line
　　The fairer part are smitten
And deem the verse must sure be fine
　　By form so graceful written.
Yet he, though proud mnidst't cheering cries –
[Though] dust from [   ] clap'd arise
Though all around him envying eyes
　　Tell him he has not toiled in vain,
Yet short the triumphs of his reign.
As winds the Pageant through the door,
His little hour of glory's o'er! –

'Mirror of Life'
(Found in the pocket of one of JEAL 's diaries)

Mirror of Life! where lie confus'dly tost
   The clustering trifles shaken from our minds,
As every worthless thing, to memory lost,
   On lunar shores a dark existence finds.

Record of facts and interests, now no more,
   Still may thy monumental* page declare,
To him who idling reads thy secrets o'er,
   How men, wise men, for deity prepare.

And, should he deem thy copious leaves a blank,
   Bid *him* his richer stores of memory show;
Tell him I danced and hunted, ate and drank,
   And came and went, as others come and go.

                         J.E. Austen.

Speen, January 1, 1822.

*Lines accompanying a pearl pin, addressed to
William Heathcote* on Friday May 17th: 1822.
On which day he came of age.*

William, A Muse I once possesed,
    A poor, but willing maid,
The inmate of a lightsome breast,
    Though not a weighty head.

She sported in the verdant bower
    Of lifes yet dewy vale,
E'er time had bade from herb & flower
    The glittering radiance fail.

She's fled; or on this day of pride,
    When, not for thee in vain,
Youth's quiet vista open's wide,
    On manhood's active plain;

Thou sh^dst. have heard her joy, her boast
    Her pride from envy free,
At seeing in my friend, what most
    Myself w^d. wish to be.

But still, though pass ungrasped away
    The wished for powers of mind;
Though fancy's blighted bud's decay,
    And leave no fruit behind.

Regard for thee, thank heaven, appears
    Less willing to depart;
Which, strengthened by the growth of years
    Watered by common hopes & fears,
Is rooted in my heart.

Winchester*
May 17: 1822

Prologue to The Sultan, acted at Ashington Parsonage* –
some time in the 19ᵗʰ Century –

Enter the Manager much distracted –

Oh! dear I am sure I don't know what to do,
There's a hole in the curtain, its coming in two.
The Sultan I fear in his feathers will fail,
That vile Bantam cock has so short a tail –
Roxalana & Elmira* have just had a brawl,
'Cause one is too short, & the other so* tall.
Ismena* pretends she has got a sore throat,
But it's only she's modest, & can't sing a note.
As for Osmyn,* poor fellow, I know he can't sing,
But I hoped he would whistle, he'll do no such thing.
The mutes will all chatter, the carver will carve,
And between them I fear they'll the manager starve.
Kind ladies & gen'men I'm ready to cry
I hope you'll applaud, or I surely shall die.

An Epilogue to the Sultan spoken by
the Author at Ashington* in Sussex on
Wednesday June 18th: 1823. before the
curtain fell, & addressed to the performers.

Are then my dreams of self importance o'er,*
Must Turkish visions swell my pride no more?
Dreams which might sager heads than mine beguile,
Of rival beauties vying for my Smile –
Dreams of three tails* – But that's a doubtful blessing,
Dreams of three wives*– that loss is most distressing.
Must I, contracted to my proper span
Shrink to the native nothingness of Man –
Sultan no more, Slave to my Slaves appear,
And, from the mightiest, bow the lowliest here?
Hard is my lot: while you, by nature's law,
In Turkish turban crowned, or English straw;
Whether you play the real, or feigned part,
Still hold your rank & empire, oer the heart;
Alone, for traitor to his sex & king,
The rebel Osmyn* joins the female ring –
In unsupported solitude, I stand,
And beg those smiles, I may not now command.
     Yes, & their coy reluctance to compel,
I here invoke them by a potent spell –
So may your Lords, when any Lords you own,
Divide, like me, the matrimonial throne.
Sultans, when all the world are gazing on,

May they with seeming sway,* command, & have it done
But when your parlours closing curtain falls,
And no strange eye may pierce the sacred walls,
May they with ease resign that seeming sway;
Let Loveliness command, & Love obey.

(1) *The Author spoke in the character of Sultan; all the other performers being Ladies.*

(2) *The character of Osmyn the only male character in the play, except the Sultan himself, was acted by Miss Warren.* Ashington.

Lines written at Bear hill Cottage, Berkshire,

Oct: 16:[th] 1824

When the sailor boy rocked on the boundless pacific,
    In some friendly Island his harbour has made,
Which mild, in its clime, & by nature prolific,
    Can cheer with it's fruits, & refresh with it's shade

2

Some sweet sunny Island, unmarked in the chart,
    Mid barrenness fertile, in solitude gay –
Whose loneliness warns him full oft to depart,
    Whose loveliness silently wooes him to stay.

3

How oft, as he seeks the earths furthest extreme,
    Oer his thoughts that lone land of enchantment will steal –
Whose transient enjoyment wo[d]. mark it a dream,
    Whose lasting impression denotes it as real –

4

How oft will he think of its beauties all wasted,
    With none to appreciate the scenes he has lost;
It's calm unenjoyed, & its treasures untasted;
    And all the vain charms of that desolate coast.

5

And thus, unexpected as some green Oasis,
    Mid a dearth[†] intellectual of many a mile;
All rich in mild manners, strong sense, & bright faces,
    This house spread to us a society isle,

6

And thus, like the Sailor, but O! not for ever!

From this newly found region of bliss must we haste;

And stern stubborn distance must far from us sever,

What is *near* in remembrance & *home* to our taste.

J.E.A.

† With one or two exceptions –

On a run from Milk hill*

Let Harmsworth* display on her long Kennel Wall
Their Trophys of racing & dipping, & all,
Let the hero of Heckfield* pursue if he will
To Illsley* the Game which he seldom can kill,
While Precious & Latimer bay at the Vine
Oh still may their Sport, & their praises be mine,
Who let few escape while the scent will but serve,
And ne'er kill'd a Fox which they did not deserve.
The Morning was windy, the Country was high,
When George* & his rattlers* to Poleswood* drew nigh,
While his hounds with "ware hare" urging still in their Ear,
[Were] thinking the Beacon Hill* rather too near,
And a substitute filling the station of Pop,*
Prepared every riotous Puppy to stop.
But as riotous Puppys there chanced to be none
He saved all his whipcord, & lost all his Fun.
That Foe to all Sporting & Sportsmen, the Gout,
Forbad the groom Squire* himself to be out,
But still round the Cover impatiently stood
A train, full as many as did any good.
While George at the Wind & the country look'd gravish,
And hallow'd Ya over, Ya! drag him up Lavish,
And Gamester encouraged in evry wood
Would have given his Tongue twenty times, if he could.
No need of encouraging hallow so shrill,
When each Tongue was proclaiming a Find on Milk hill,
And there scarcely was time for one softly, before
The cover was elft* to be enter'd no more
And the various groups standing still by the side
Were forced in a hurry to scramble & ride,

The talkers of politics stop'd consultation
And thought of themselves rather more than the Nation,
And the Croakers* just settled, there could be no scent
When the Fox was view'd off, & away they all went,
They went, & some few, I'm afraid chanced to find,
That the farther they rode, they*

Prologue spoken by Edward* in the character of
'Scrub of the Company,'
Sutton, September 10, 1851

(Puts his head through the curtain and looks round at the audience.)

Kind neighbours and friends I've a secret to tell;

I fancy this acting will turn out a 'Sell.'*

You'll find that there's nothing worth coming to see,

    (Comes forward from behind the curtains.)

Not a genius amongst them – unless it be *'Me.'*

For the ladies, poor creatures, to give them their due,

They've kept the whole house in a worry and stew;

And however *they* fail, I will boldly protest

They are doing the very *outside of their best.*

But as for the 'gemmen,' they have not a chance

They will do nothing well till they get to the dance;

They are safe* to break down – and shall I tell you why?

Perhaps you imagine they're modest and shy?

No – they're only too bold – the truth is, *they won't try;*

With their billiards all night, and their shooting all day,

They can't spare a moment to study the play.

They might do it much better, no doubt, if they chose,

But they'll scarce take the trouble to put on their clothes;

They will never rehearse, but by snatches and bits,

And they've plagued the poor manager out of her wits;

They *will* trust to their mem'ry – but mem'ry is frail,

They *will* trust to their talents – you'll see how they fail.

It was but this morning my lubber!y* brother

Vow'd he'd so many parts he would not take another;

So he put on poor *me,* without notice, to speak

What he might have been learning the whole of the week!

I'm pretty well used to the weight of his fist, –
But it's rather too hard in his stead to be hissed.
So since breakfast I've had to learn all Mr. Winkle –*
But hush! – in two minutes you'll hear the bell tinkle,
And as I'm an oppressed and ill-used little chap,
Hiss the others and welcome, but give me a clap!

(Exit through the curtains, clapping his hands.)

Œnigma* *written at Chawton*
in the summer 1820

Ye Nymphs of Chawton* to my lay attend,
And own your bitterest foe, or firmest friend –
For wether sporting oer the level green*
Where hearts are lost & won, my form is seen,
Or ranged amid the ranks of massive war,
Of three strong brethren* most effective far,
Kings trunkiess heads, my warfares fruits you see,
Or ruined damsels mourn their sports with me;
Mighty to save, yet potent to destroy,
The fairest hands receive my aid with joy:
And while all round me feel their dubious way,
Light is my conquest, & my work is play;
Though lines engraved around my front* evince,
I ne'er have failed in duty to my Prince,*
Yet at my feet must royal consorts fall
Nor Kings disdain to answer to my call;
While trembling hearts, and clubs that strike not, shew –
I own no equal, & I fear no foe –

J.E.A.

85

Enigma

What when the golden Age was gone
Was left divine on Earth alone?
Midst sorrow's seats content to stray
And only scared by guilt away
What stronger rises in the breast
By disappointment most deprest?
As springs, through stones upon them cast
Gush life as freely & as fast
What when we groan with present ill
Still moulds the future as it will?
The lover's food, the parent's joy,
The cheerer of his home-sick boy.

What loves the anchor,* & the oar
And in the Horizon paints the shore?
And whispers to the soul distrest
A calmer port, a longer rest
Like charity all griefs would cure*
Like charity can much endure*
What best the parting spirit cheers
Checks the surviving mourner's tears
And mounting to its native skies
Melts into actual bliss, and dies.

JEA

Charades

My 1st. is oft done by old persons & Boys,
By the old with themselves, by the young with their toys
My second's adapted for mortification
And my whole for my second's the best preparation.

I.EA.

My 1st. is of nature, my 2^{d} of art
    And tho' each for the other seems formed
Yet Men, whom my 2^{d}. delight to the heart
    By my 1st. very seldom are charmed

2.

They will use the poor creature enough to be sure
    As a slave might be used by a Turk
To wash out their dishes, or scrub up their floor
    To keep out of sight, & to work.

3

Yet my whole on their table must often appear
    And midst wassail & wine take it's station
Where it stands unpolluted, an emblem most clear
    Of purity placed in temptation.

I.E.A.

1

Shake my 1st., & to you in return it will give
  A good shake, perhaps rather too rough;
If you suffer my 2d a twelvemonth to live,
  You will find it grown quite big enough.

2

My whole stands all day with its back to the wall
  A sad gossip as ever you'll meet,
Knows the first of each robbery, concert, or Ball,
  And tells every soul in the street.

I.E.A.

My first, to aid the works of Man,
  From heaven a present came;
And yet this Slave, do all we can,
  We cannot catch or tame.

2

For now t'is on the mountains brow,
  And now t'is on the wave,
Now sports in beauty's bower, and now
  Sighs o'er the maniac's grave.

3

My second, like my first, I'm sure
  From heaven its essence drew,
As soft, as fragrant, & as pure,
  Say not as changeful too.

4

My whole explores Earth's deepest stores,
    And draws, like wisdom, up
The purest draught, that e'er is quaffed,
    From mortal's varying Cup.

Compton*
Aug:st 23
1823

My 1st. should be long,
    My 1st should be strong,
My 1st should he done altogether
    My next should be deep
    If you mean it to keep
Your potatoes in cold frosty weather

2.

    My whole dressed in red,*
    With a high grotesque head,
Will against pride & vanity speak
    And 'gainst idleness too,
    Tho' its own work t'will do
Very seldom, above once a week.

JEA.

My 1st, tho' now no chicken thought
    Has not her conquests ended
You'll meet her still at many a Court
    By Coxcombs still attended

2

My next, when you have pears to buy
    Is no uncommon Measure;
But woe to pairs my whole comes nigh
    Sworn foe to peace & pleasure

3.

That whole's a word which all Men shun
    Yet why should they eschew it?
I never found a *single* one,
    Who from experience knew it.

JEA.

Bouts-Rimés

Gay – Trouble – Bay – Ray – Double.

In days of yore, when 'Prentice gay
    Fell into debt and trouble,
He blackened his face and he mounted his bay
And stopped coaches and six, with their cumbrous array
    And for his debts got double.*

'Your hounds are much too fresh and gay,
    They'll bring you into trouble;
They'll flash at larks – at sheepdogs bay,
Far from the scent they'll yelp and stray,
    But never hunt a double.

Sleep – Creep – Chatter – Turn – Burn – Batter.

Hark! where those shadowy woodlands sleep,
And murmuring waters slowly creep,
Picknicking parties chatter:
Indignant from the sight I turn,
Ye gods! by that romantic burn,
    They're frying eggs and batter!*

[*Fright – Crack – Night – Lack.*]

"Oh: Betty what makes me look such a fright?
Sure the old mirror has got a crack
"Why Maam, you'll be fifty, next Saturday night
And beauty will wane – a-lack – a-lack".

J.E.A.L.

Page – Muster – Age – Cluster.

How thick on the heraldic page
    Ancestral honours muster;
Warrior and sage, of every age,
    A rich and varied cluster.

This man was the eighth Henry's page
    At the Cloth of Gold's grand muster;
On that, the Statesman of his age,
    Honours and titles cluster.

Round yon fair girl, like sweet Anne Page,*
    The loves and graces muster;
She wins a prince's appanage*
    And courtiers round her cluster.

But turn we to a sadder page
    The churchyard's silent muster
Brave, fair and sage, of every age,*
    'Tis there at last they cluster.

Power – Lot – Flower – Dower – Cot.

They who have climbed the steep ascent of power,
    Even at its summit murmur at their lot;
They find it bare of verdure, fruit and flower,
    And empty fame remains their only dower,
While nameless blessings deck the sheltered cot.

Leg – Beg – Pond – Bond,

I tied up my leg
And I set out to beg:
But got ducked in a pond
For an old vag-abond.

J.E.A.L.

Ditch – Witch – Cottage – Pottage.

1.

Fishing tadpoles from a ditch,
1 saw a gaunt & hungry witch;
Following softly to her cottage
I watched her mix her horrid pottage.

2.

She threw in toads & newts from the ditch,
Tadpoles or leeches – she cared not which,
Cobwebs & spiders she swept from her cottage,
And they all simmered up in her savoury pottage.

J.E.A.L.

Whistle – Day – Thistle -- Pay

Some one must pay for every whistle;*
    See, upon St. Andrew's Day,
Balston,* gorgeous with his thistle,*
    But who's the boy that has to pay?

J.E.

Verse – Able – Nurse – Purse – Fable

Faint echoes of departed verse
My memory to recal is able
As chanted by my good old nurse
Knitting that everlasting purse,
    Combining moral still with fable.

J.E.A.L. Feb 1859

Rate – Grate – Leisure – Grass – Pass -- Treasure.

    What does that fair girl's heart commemorate
    This Holy Eve, within the Convent's grate?
Do saintly thoughts engross her consecrated leisure?
    No -- homeward far o'er forest, rock and grass,
    Her innocent thoughts free and unbounded pass
To parents, brothers, friends or some more deeply cherished
                      treasure.

J.E.

Kind – Mind – Nation – Still – Will – Ration.

1871.
    With victories of every .kind
    Gambetta* charms the Gallic mind
      And cheers the expectant nation.
His words and promises are still
That if they *have not* won, they *will,*
    But it wants corroboration.

J.E.

Town – Live – Brown – Gown – Shiver.

Mr. Woodhouse:
"My dear, I'm sure your end of town
   Is dangerous to your liver;
The gruel is made by far too brown;
Why will you wear that flimsy gown?
   That open door too makes me shiver."

J.E.

Miss Bates:
"So very kind -- going up to town --
   What's in that tray? Oh! some calf's liver;
I wondered what could look so brown,
Dear Mrs. Elton -- what a gown!
   Yes ma'am, it snows, you well may shiver."

J.E.

Noun Verses

Question: *Which of our dogs is best, next to Sentinel?*
Noun: *Humbug.*

> If merits should he rightly reckoned,
> To Sentinel* there is no second;
> 'Twere humbug to assign a place
> To dogs of an inferior race,
> As if much difference there could be
> 'Twixt Tweedledum and Tweedledee.*

J.E.

Question: *Why must every white have its black, and every sweet its sour?*
Noun: *Cover.*

I can't tell why, but so it is,
    All good is dashed with evil,
Since sorrow first invaded bliss,
    And Eden held the Devil.

A kitten soon becomes a cat,
    A husband grows the lover,
A mile of open* lands you at
    A dozen miles of cover.

J.E.

Question: *Do the English dance or sing best?*
Noun: *Sticking-plaister.*

To learn to dance,
You must go to France,
And much the same thing
If you wish to sing,
But to stick to a point like sticking-plaister
I'd rather learn of an English master.

J.E.

Question: *Which are you for, North or South?*
Noun: *Rose.*

Between the Red Rose and the White,*
    Or Cavalier and Roundhead,
I've some idea of wrong and right
    On truth and reason grounded:
But North and South have wrong and right
    Between them so confounded
That I confess my judgment quite
    Skedaddled and astounded.

J.E.

Question: *'Why are Pigs so dear?'*
Noun: *Parrot*

    [1] James Dodd loquitur.

    Says Mr. Parrot unto me

    'James -- why *is* Pigs so dear? says he;

    To Mr. Parrot then says I,

    ''Tis Sir, because you want to buy,

    But they'll be cheaper, I can tell,

    Whenever you have Pigs to sell.'

[1] An eccentric old servant of his great-uncle, Mr Leigh-Perrot, who always called his master 'Mr. Parrot'. [Mary Augusta Austen-Leigh]

Question: *'Which shall we take in, the "Cornhill"* or the "Monthly Packet"?*
Noun: *Butterfly*

    Between the Gnat or Butterfly

    And such ephemeral things

    Insects, or Magazines, I'd try

    The one that buzzes harmless by,

    And not the one that stings.

Question: *Why is a newspaper like a kite?*
Noun: *Eggshell.*

The case lies in an Eggshell;* the Times, like a kite
Soars high for its prey, & comes down with a bite

                J.E.A. Leigh

Question: *What becomes of all the pins in the world?*
Noun: *Boar's head.*

Distressing thought! Where – where -- who knows,
Do shades of pins defunct repose?
The pin that fastened Jael's tent*
And through Sisera's temples went?
Pins, numerous once, now scarce, and rare,
Which decked the Roman matron's hair?
Pins mediaeval somewhere sleep,
Used at the "Boar's head"* in Eastcheap;
And still, as older grows the world,
Pin after pin to fate is hurled.
Who knows? I end as I begin:
I neither know nor care a pin!

J.E.

Question: *Do you take snuff?*
Noun: *Fox.*

As seldom take I snuff, alack!
    As Robert* takes a fox;
Although for show he hunts a pack,
    And I display a box.

J.E.

Question: *Why does the Cock crow?*
Noun: *Sugar*

You ask me why Cock a doodle does crow? –
If you'd pay me with *sugar* plums I do not know.

J.E.A.L. for Willy.

BIBLIOGRAPHY

Unpublished

'Fugitive Pieces' Small album in hand of JEAL with 48 numbered pages, pp. 3-4 and 25-26 removed, 28-29 blank, 46-47 numbered twice. Autograph signature on inside cover. Isel Hall, Cumbria.

'Fugitive Pieces 2nd' Album similar to above, but with fewer than half the pages used. Hampshire Record Office, Austen-Leigh archive 23M93/86/5/2.

HRO Other MSS in the Hampshire Record Office, Austen-Leigh archive.

Gilson Small album in unidentified hand, c. 1830, containing 44 riddles and charades by members of the Austen family. Also other MSS. David Gilson Esq.

Silhouettes The silhouette pictures are from a scrapbook, bound in green with gold tooling and gilt edges to the pages, which also contains various drawings. It bears the bookplate of Cholmeley Austen-Leigh, JEAL's eldest son, and an inscription by him: 'This scrapbook was made for me about the years 1835-6 by my dear Father. Most of the black cuttings out & drawings were done by his own hand; & some of the latter, as I well remember, on scraps of paper, while I was construing Latin or reading history to him. After his death, Sept. 8. 1874, 1 had the little book bound. C.A.L. Nov. 1874.' Isel Hall, Cumbria.

Published

All references to the novels of Jane Austen are to the Oxford Illustrated Jane Austen, ed. R.W. Chapman, Oxford, 1923. The Juvenilia and other minor works were first collected in vol. VI of the Oxford edition as *Minor Works*, ed. Chapman, 1954, rev. B.C. Southam, 1969.

References to *Jane Austen's Letters* are to the 3rd edition, ed. Deirdre Le Faye, Oxford, 1995.

Austen, Caroline Mary Craven, *My Aunt Jane Austen,* Jane Austen Society, 1952.

–, *Reminiscences of Caroline Austen,* ed. Deirdre Le Faye, Jane Austen Society, 1986.

Austen-Leigh, J.E., *A Memoir of Jane Austen,* London, 1870.

–, *Recollections of the Early Days of the Vine Hunt,* London, 1865.

Austen-Leigh, Mary Augusta, *James Edward Austen Leigh: A Memoir,* privately printed, 1911.

Austen-Leigh, R.A., *Austen Papers,* London, 1942.

Jane Austen Society, *Collected Reports,* 5 vols, 1949-2000, continuing.

Lane, Maggie, *Jane Austen's Family: Through Five Generations,* London, 1984.

Le Faye, Deirdre, *Jane Austen: A Family Record,* 2nd edn., Cambridge, 2004.

Selwyn, David, ed., *Jane Austen: Collected Poems and verse of the Austen family,* Manchester, 1996.

–, ed., *The Complete Poems of James Austen,* Chawton, 2003.

NOTES

7 THE NECK OF VEAL Source: autograph MS 'Fugitive Pieces'. The six-year-old demonstrates a remarkably precocious gift for making epigrams.

8 TO PAPA WITH A KNIFE Source: autograph MS 'Fugitive Pieces'. Another MS, with minor variants, on a separate sheet (HRO 23M93/86/5/1) found among letters to James Austen is presumably the one JEAL gave to his father; the paper has a watermark of 1810, which gives a clue to the date of composition.
if a knife you give away: 'The commonest modem superstition about knives is that, because they are sharp-cutting, they sever love or friendship when given as a present. They should never be accepted without something being given in exchange.' (E. & M.A. Radford, ed. Hole, *Encyclopaedia of Superstitions*, London, 1961)

9 TO MAMMA Source: autograph MS 'Fugitive Pieces'. A somewhat equivocal tribute, perhaps, to his mother, described by Jane Austen as 'in the main *not a* liberal-minded Woman' *(Letters,* pp. 340-41). JEAL must have thought the poem scarcely did her justice (see the later verse with the same title, p. 53).
Ramsbury Where JEAL went to school (see below, p.106).

10 THE PATRIOT Source: autograph MS 'Fugitive Pieces'. The 'Patriot Smalbone' from 'great Dean Town', riding at full gallop to Warwick, is strongly reminiscent of John Gilpin. In his *Memoir of Jane Austen* JEAL cites Cowper as one of aunt's favourite poets and 'The Diverting History of John Gilpin' (1782) would have been familiar to him from an early age; both in rhythm and tone the echoes are unmistakable.
great Dean Town James Austen was his father's curate at Deane, the neighbouring parish to Steventon, from 1792 until 1805; JEAL was bom there in 1798. In 1801 the family moved to Steventon rectory on the Revd George Austen's retirement to Bath. The spelling 'Dean' was used on contemporary maps, though not by Jane Austen in her letters, except when referring to Dean Gate.
Smalbone Daniel Smallbone, of Deane, had eight children, of whom two, Mary and Betsy, were successively nursemaids to JEAL's younger sister, Caroline.
Mrs Liney Unidentified.

12 THE RACES Source: autograph MS 'Fugitive Pieces'. Following a gleeful account of the moral degeneracy to which the races lead, the last line makes an amusing volte-face.

the new 'pointed race: started in July 1753, the Kempshott Races on Basingstoke Down were held annually until 1788; they were resumed in 1811, and finally abandoned in 1829.

13 FOX HUNTING COMMENCED Source: autograph MS 'Fugitive Pieces'. Both JEAL and his father were very fond of hunting. James Austen, having hunted from an early age, gave it up when approaching middle age, but returned to it for a few seasons when his son took it up at the age of fifteen. They hunted with the Hampshire Hunt and with Mr Chute's hounds from The Vyne; many stories of the hunts and their members were included in JEAL's *Recollections of the Early Days of the Vine Hunt.* James Austen wrote an amusing poem about his son's disappointment at not being allowed to hunt one day while he was being prepared for entrance to Winchester (see *The Complete Poems of James Austen,* p. 67). In the present poem, adopting the voice of the fox, the young poet cleverly deploys the rain to spell danger in two ways: by bringing the races to an end, thus prompting the beginning of the hunting season, and by ensuring that the scent will be good; and he incidentally gets in a good jibe at the Methodists, undoubtedly reflecting his father's opinion of them.

[not] MS: no.

famous Excellent. The fox is ironically permitted a colloquialism reflecting the relish expressed by his pursuers.

14 ON THE DUMMER HARRIERS Source: autograph MS 'Fugitive Pieces'. A few miles south-east of Steventon is the Village of Dummer, where the Terry family, friends of the Austens, lived at Dummer House. Stephen Terry, with whom Jane Austen danced, was a keen hunting squire and in later life kept a series of journals, published as *The Diaries of Dummer* (ed. A.M.W. Stirling, 1934), which recorded his experiences in the field. By then he was hunting foxes, but in earlier days, like other neighbours of the Austens, he kept harriers: although fox-hunting had grown in popularity during the 18th century, it did not overtake hare-hunting until Victorian times. At the period when JEAL wrote this poem the harriers belonged to Stephen's father, Thomas Terry.

John Presumably a groom at Steventon. Probably not John Bond, the farm bailiff, who by the time the poem was written was in his seventies; possibly his son, also John, though he is known to have become at some stage a gamekeeper.

bounty Despite the absence of a capital letter, this is presumably one of the hounds.

Canning Possibly Mr Terry's huntsman.

[fail] MS: fear.

hun[t]sman MS: hunsman.

he A slip for 'she'.

I came out a view The exact sense is not quite clear.

pussey Pussy was used as a proper name for the hare.

17 DIRT & SLIME Source: autograph MS 'Fugitive Pieces'. A copy in the hand of Cholmeley Austen-Leigh (HRO 23M93/86/5/1) supplies a date of 1813. The fourteen-year-old schoolboy affectionately sends up his father's proto-Romantic nature poetry; in later life he lovingly made careful transcriptions of it.

Kintbury The Revd Fulwar Craven Fowle, a close friend of James Austen from childhood, was vicar of Kintbury, Berkshire.

Some very pretty verses 'Home. Written on returning from Kintbury -- Sepr: 1812'. The poem begins:

> Through Berkshire's lanes & hedgerows green,
> When, the spreading oaks between,
> Peeps the landscape's varied charm,
> Cornfield, mead, or sheltered farm,
> Intervening copse & heath
> In gay confusion, & beneath
> The shelter of each sloping hill,
> Many a little nameless rill
> Through alders dark, or willows gray,
> Or rushes, works its tangled way;
> Hasty through these fair scenes I passed...

Though James Austen characteristically describes with an artist's eye the landscape through which he passes, the concern of the poem is with the attraction of home. See *The Complete Poems of James Austen*, pp. 44-46.

pleased as punch Nicely out of keeping with the elevated tone of the Muses.

bays In classical times poets were crowned with garlands of bay leaves.

hillock MS: hilloc.

ran the heel Ran back on the scent.

19 ADDRESS TO BUONAPARTE Source: autograph MS 'Fugitive Pieces'. Napoleon's retreat from Moscow in the bitter winter of 1812 resulted in the near annihilation of the French army. JEAL fiercely attacks the 'tyrant' in this poem, which seems to be incomplete.

Gallia's Land France. Gallia, the Latin for Gaul, was an 18th-century poeticism.

Scythia's plains Scythia was the ancient name for a large part of European and Asiatic Russia.

20 THE SCHOOL-BOYS WISH Source: autograph MS 'Fugitive Pieces'. I am very grateful to Janet Clarke for deciphering the poem. Her version runs thus:

> We wish it was time
> To go home
> Glad we would be
> A Pound to see
> And what a bit of fun
> At Christmas would come
> Misery would go away
> Bright and merry we'd stay
> And Ramsbury we
> Never again would see

It is possible, however, that 'me' in ll. 1 and 3, and 'mibredy' in 1. 9, are in the singular, since the title suggests one boy, who is of course JEAL himself.

Ramsburruddub Ramsbury, Wilts. 'On 12th August [18121 my brother went to school, at Mr Meyrick's of Ramsbury, my father taking him there, and staying a night in Kintbury.' *(Reminiscences of Caroline Austen,* p. 26) The Revd Edward Graves Meyrick (1781-1839), vicar of Ramsbury, ran the school founded by his father in the vicarage, though as it grew it was largely under the supervision of his brother, the Revd Arthur Meyrick, in his house Bodorgan (now Ramsbury Hill). JEAL remained there until June 1813, with an interruption for the anticipated Christmas holiday. (See Chris Viveash, 'Placed at school', Jane Austen Society *Collected Reports* vol. V, 1996-2000, pp. 250-52, and, for details of Ramsbury, Barbara Croucher, *The Village in the Valley,* Ramsbury, 1986.)

21 TO ANNA, A RIDDLE Source: autograph MS 'Fugitive Pieces'. In this verse JEAL ingeniously combines the form of a riddle (to which the solution is of course a looking-glass) with a graceful compliment to his sister Anna.

this writer's very self the writer is being modest, since he would certainly not have seen a 'hideous face' when he looked in the glass: portraits and accounts of contemporaries attest to his having been very good-looking.
[a] MS: &.

22 TO ANNA Source: autograph MS 'Fugitive Pieces'.
Returning from the busy Race Anna spent the summer of 1812 with her grandmother and aunts at Chawton, returning to Steventon at the end of September.

23 THE FLOWER Source: autograph MS: 'Fugitive Pieces'. Jane Anna Elizabeth, James Austen's daughter by his first wife, was born on 15 April 1793. The tone of JEAL's tribute, moving between tender sentiment and gentle moralising, is reminiscent of similar poems by his father (see for example below, p. 114); though it is interesting that while James addressed poems to his two younger children, he seems to have written nothing for Anna.
your Edwards sake JEAL was always known in the family as Edward, just as Jane Anna Elizabeth was Anna.
Th'unconscious month Nature, invoked as an expression of love in the flower, is, so far as the progress of time is concerned, unfeeling.
where will Anna then be found? This is possibly a sly reference to the verse Jane Austen addressed to Anna, a few years earlier, when the latter had briefly been engaged to the Revd Michael Terry, a match that her parents opposed. In it she described her niece as having a mind 'unconfined / Like any vast savannah', compared the breadth of her 'fancy' to Lake Ontario and her wit descending on people to 'famed Niagara's Fall', and reckoned her judgment 'thick, black, profound, / Like transatlantic groves' (see *Jane Austen: Collected Poems and verse of the Austen Family*, pp. 12-13). JEAL's abrupt halt in the travelogue after the one reference to the Cumbrian mountains would undoubtedly have caused a smile at Steventon -- and no doubt at Chawton too.
At Steventon she will not be: this suggests that the poem was written in 1814, since Anna married Ben Lefroy in the November of that year.
a cottage oer my head At sixteen JEAL was old enough to know better than to write so carelessly!
[Then] MS: The.
this sweet flower The return to the flower, through pictured memories, is deftly done and the repeat of the opening couplet, with the intensification of 'Then love', gives a satisfying shape to the poem.

25 ODE OF HORACE IMITATED Source: autograph MS 'Fugitive Pieces'. Adopting the practice of many 18th-century poets, JEAL takes a classical poem as the basis of his own work. Horace in Odes Book I Ode I, dedicated to his patron Maecenas, disclaims the aspirations of charioteer, politician, farmer, merchant, sybarite, soldier and hunter, prizing only the rewards of the writer of lyric poetry. Substituting his father for Maecenas and the prospect of a prize at Oxford for Polyhymnia's lyre, JEAL follows Horace closely.

patriotic Pitt William Pitt the Younger, prime minister 1783-1801 and 1804-06. His alliance with Austria, Russia and Sweden against Napoleon ended at Austerlitz, and he died on hearing the news, saying 'Oh my country! How I leave my country!'

Attalus A king of Pergamos; the allusion is taken from Horace.

merchant MS: merchan.

Oxford JEAL is thinking ahead: he did not leave Ramsbury for Winchester until 1814 and went up to Exeter College, Oxford only in 1816, winning a Founder's Kin Craven Scholarship the following year.

27 TO MISS J AUSTEN Source: autograph MS 'Fugitive Pieces'. Following the publication of *Pride and Prejudice* in January 1813, the identity of the author of this and the earlier *Sense and Sensibility* (both published anonymously) gradually became known, largely as a result of Henry Austen's pride in his sister's work; until then it had been concealed from the younger members of the family.

Butcher Pile: The *National Commercial Directory* for Berkshire, Buckinghamshire, Gloucestershire, Hampshire and Oxfordshire (1830) lists a George Pyle, butcher and baker, in Overton and a Thomas Pyle, butcher, in Whitchurch; one of them may have visited Steventon to do some slaughtering. JEAL's robust simile is comically out of keeping with the tone of this tribute to his Aunt's literary achievement.

Mrs Jennings … Ferrars In *S&S*.

cottages For Robert Ferrars's grandiose conception of a 'cottage' see *S&S* vol. II, ch. 14, pp. 251-52.

Mr Collins ... Lady de Burgh In *P&P*. JEAL's misspelling is noteworthy and perhaps indicates that he had heard the novel read aloud.

Sir William Sir William Welby was a cousin of Mrs Leigh-Perrot and also father-in-law of her niece Wilhelmina, whom in 1801 Jane Austen reported as 'singing Duetts with the Prince of Wales' *(Letters*, p. 74). Mrs Leigh-Perrot and her husband were fond of their nephew James, and her talk of Sir William and other grand acquaintances would no doubt have become something of a joke among the younger members of his family.

becoming his *wife* The Princess of Wales had been the subject of much discussion since the publication in the newspapers earlier in the year of a letter from her to the Prince Regent protesting at his refusal to allow her visiting rights to their daughter, the Princess Charlotte; on 16 February 1813 Jane Austen had written to Martha Lloyd: 'I suppose all the World is sitting in Judgement on the Princess of Wales's Letter. Poor Woman, I shall support her as long as I can, because she is a Woman, & because I hate her Husband...' *(Letters*, p. 208).

28 THE LION & THE FOX Source: autograph MS 'Fugitive Pieces'. Mrs George Austen had written verse fables, in the manner John Gay (see *Jane Austen: Collected Poems and verse of the Austen Family*, pp. 31-2); here her grandson makes use of the form to depict the behaviour of a little girl, no doubt drawing on his observations of his sister Caroline.

he[r] MS: he.

Ramsbury See note above, p. 106.

29 ON THE DEATH OF L B WITHER ESQ[RE]. Source: autograph MS 'Fugitive Pieces'. Lovelace Bigg-Wither, the father of Jane and Cassandra Austen's friends Elizabeth, Catherine and Alethea Bigg, had provided a home at Manydown for Elizabeth and William following the early death of her husband, the Revd William Heathcote, in March 1802. Since the boy had been less than a year old when his father died, his grandfather must have been a very important figure in his early life, and it is his grief that the young JEAL tries to lessen in the poem, by reminding his friend that he will eventually meet his 'gransire' again in Heaven.

you bid me write JEAL and William both kept books in which they wrote poems and obviously showed them to each other; when in 1808 Catherine Bigg married the Revd Herbert Hill, William, distraught at losing his sister, wrote 'Sweet creature parted from all her friends but one', to which JEAL added 'Who in kindness is excelled by none' (see Robert Heathcote Lawrence, 'Jane Austen at Manydown', Jane Austen Society *Collected Reports* vol. IV, 1986-95, p. 347).

School At this time JEAL and William were at Ramsbury (see note above, p. 106).

God (from whom all bounties flow) Cf. 'Praise God, from whom all blessings flow' (Bishop Thomas Ken, 'Morning and Evening Hymn').

31 TO MANYDOWN Source: autograph MS 'Fugitive Pieces'. Manydown Park, near Worting, Hampshire, was the home of the Bigg-Wither family (see note above, p. 109). Elizabeth Heathcote (neé Bigg) returned there after the early death of her husband in 1802; her son William (1801-1881) was a close friend of JEAL, who retained happy memories of visits to the house. In a poem that has echoes of Goldsmith's *The Deserted Village* (1770), the destruction of the old gardens as the new owner 'improves' the estate is contrasted with the conviction that no such unfortunate changes will occur in William's character.

Sweet Manydown Cf. Goldsmith's 'Sweet Auburn, loveliest village of the plain'.

pease Sweet peas.

breard More usually braird: first shoots of a plant.

thy late/And revd master Lovelace Bigg-Wither, who died on 24 February 1813 (see 'On the death of L B Wither Esqre.', p. 000).

he who fills his place Harris Bigg-Wither (1781-1833) returned to Manydown on the death of his father. Some ten years earlier, on the evening of 2 December 1802, Harris had proposed to and been accepted by Jane Austen, only to find the next morning that she had changed her mind. His 'improvements' and JEAL's dislike of them (which was presumably shared by his family) recall Fanny Price's regret at Mr Rushworth's proposed alterations at Sotherton; Jane Austen was working on *Mansfield Park* during 1813.

[l] Omitted in MS.

33 TO MISS C. CRAVEN Source: autograph MS 'Fugitive Pieces'. A new maturity comes into JEAL's verse with this tribute, in which the poet, unable to enter into the spirit of 'mirth and revelry' characteristic of the life led by the young lady, 'immured' as he is with his schoolbooks, allows his 'volumes antique of ancient lore' to inspire him in a mock-classical fable. Venus, in response to Cupid's complaint that the world has grown so mercenary that it no longer values love, produces a being so beautiful that no one could fail to adore her. Charlotte Craven (1798-1877) was the cousin of JEAL's mother, Mary Lloyd. and lived in the village of Speen, one mile west of Newbury, Berks; she was at school in London when Jane Austen visited her in May 1813 and wrote: 'She looks very well & her hair is done up with an elegance to do credit to any Education. Her manners are as unaffected & pleasing as ever....I was shewn up stairs into a draw^g room, where she came to me, & the appearance of the room, so totally un-school-like, amused me very much. It was full of all the modem Elegancies---& if it had not been for some naked Cupids over the Mantelpiece, which must be a fine study for Girls, one should never have Smelt Instruction.' *(Letters, p. 211)*

these walls JEAL had just entered Winchester College.

[ply'd] The word is unclear in the MS.

virtue 'Virtues' would read better here.

36 TO MRS B. LEFROY. ON HER WEDDING DAY Source: autograph MS 'Fugitive Pieces'. Anna Lefroy (1793-1872) was James Austen's daughter by his first wife, Anne Mathew. She and JEAL were close and whereas James is not known to have written any poems for her though he did for his other two children, her brother wrote several. She married Benjamin Lefroy at Steventon, on 8 November 1814.

November, I will love thee still JEAL echoes a poem by his father, 'April. 1805 To Mary', in which James Austen expresses his fondness for the month of April because it contained the birthday of his (second) wife, Mary Lloyd, JEAL's mother:

> ...all inconstant as thou art,
> With sunny morn & evening chill,
> April, I will love thee still
>
> *(The Complete Poems of James Austen, p. 33)*

Thou first beheldst me breathing here JEAL was born 17 November 1798. The two occasions -- his birthday and Anna's wedding day -- are neatly combined at the end of the poem.

38 A LETTER TO MISS CAROLINE AUSTEN Source: autograph MS HRO 23M93/66/2/1. This is an actual letter sent by JEAL while he was at Winchester to his ten year-old sister Caroline. A poem written by James Austen to Cassandra at more or less the same age ('The Rash Resolution', *The Complete Poems of James Austen*, p. 11) makes an interesting comparison in tone; whereas James seeks to teach his little sister a precept -- that one shouldn't say one will do a thing unless one can be sure of doing it -- JEAL writes in a spirit of pure fun, adopting the role of knight, in which he offers her a challenge, to write back to him (a challenge that she appears to have accepted, since a 'Letter in verse to my brother at Winchester 1815' is among the early writings that she burnt in 1871 [*Reminiscences*, p. 67]).

Saturday night The postmark on the letter supplies the date: 24 February 1815.

Red Button In the Chinese Empire, the highest rank of mandarin wore a red button in his cap.

Demosthenes The Athenian orator, c.384-322 BC, author of the *Philippics*.
Mr Croft The postmaster.
Ashengrove Ashen Grove Copse, 1 mile south of Steventon.
Truelove One of Mr Chute's hounds.
Harp The harp, as opposed to the fortepiano which Jane Austen played, was an instrument favoured by fashionable young ladies, and it is interesting that James and Mary Austen bought one for Caroline.
The Horses Donkey & the Cow There was still a little farming done from Steventon rectory when James Austen lived there, though he no longer had Cheesedown Farm, which his father had worked.
Dora and Lady Julia Presumably Caroline's dolls.

40 ON WESTMINSTER ABBEY Source: autograph MS 'Fugitive Pieces'. The tone of the poem is somewhat callow in its contrast between the patriotic Pitt and the 'Rable selfish wild & rude' whom he 'toiled to Save', but there is a certain sophistication in the idea that the worn tomb of a medieval knight allows the mind to imagine him more fully than the memorial to a modem statesman, our knowledge of whose 'every crime' contradicts 'the Sculptured praise'.
Nature's boast Perhaps in the sense that time has naturally eroded the man-made sculpture.
Bacons modern stone MS: 'modest' cancelled. The memorial to William Pitt the Elder, Earl of Chatham (1708-1778), twice Prime Minister, by John Bacon (1740-1799) is 33 feet high; over figures of Ocean, Earth, Prudence and Fortitude stands the figure of Pitt delivering an oration.
Sir Barnard Assuming that JEAL has a real monument in mind, he is probably referring to the tomb of Sir Bernard Brocas (1330?-1395) in the Chapel of St Edmund; Brocas was a favourite knight of Edward the 'Black Prince' and subsequently chamberlain to Anne, Queen of England. The inscription reads: 'Here lies Bernard Brocas, soldier, one-time chamberlain to Queen Anne of England: upon whose soul may God look graciously. Amen.' It was repaired in the 18th century, when a longer inscription was added.
Bustos Portrait busts.
Too MS: 'More' cancelled.
Bust of Pitt The monument to Pitt the Younger (see note above, p. 000) by Richard Westmacott is placed above the west door of the Abbey; it portrays Pitt declaiming while the Muse of History records his words and the figure of Anarchy crouches at his feet. But JEAL may be referring to Bacon's monument to Pitt the Elder.

a Nations gift The inscription reads: 'This monument is erected by Parliament, to William Pitt, Son of William, Earl of Chatham, in testimony of gratitude for the eminent public services, and of regret for the irreparable loss of that great and disinterested minister. He died on the 23 January 1806, in the 47th year of his age.' If, however, JEAL means Pitt the Elder, the inscription is: 'Erected by the King and Parliament as a testimony to the virtues and ability of William Pitt, Earl of Chatham; during whose administration in the reigns of George the Second and George the Third Divine Providence exalted Great Britain to an height of prosperity and glory unknown to any former age. Born 15 November 1708. Died 11 May 1778.

greedy MS: 'greedy' (or perhaps 'gready') cancelled, but no other word has been substituted.

43 THE WOOD WALK ... TO ANNA Source: autograph MS: 'Fugitive Pieces'. JEAL ends his first little volume of poems with an elegiac piece which, in recalling a place that had meant a great deal to him and his sister in the past but which they no longer see together, seems to be a farewell to childhood. Anna, now married, visits Steventon while he is away at Winchester; he can only look forward to the summer, when he will also go to the Wood Walk and dream that they are there again as children, until, in a charmingly prosaic touch, he is woken up by a gnat. In her account of Steventon rectory, Anna described the place: 'At one end this Terrace communicated by a small gate with what was termed, "the Wood Walk", which, winding through clumps of underwood, and over hung by tall Elm trees, skirted the upper side of the "Home Meadow"' (Lefroy MS, quoted in Jane Austen Society *Collected Reports* vol. II, 1966-75, pp. 245-46). More rhapsodically, JEAL wrote in the *Memoir*: '...the chief beauty of Steventon consisted in its hedgerows. A hedgerow, in that country, does not mean a thin formal line of quickset, but an irregular border of copse-wood and timber, often wide enough to contain within it a winding footpath, or a rough cart track.... Two such hedgerows radiated, as it were, from the parsonage garden. One, a continuation of the turf terrace, proceeded westward, forming the southern boundary of the home-meadows; and. was formed into a rustic shrubbery, with occasional seats, entitled "The Wood Walk".' (Ch. 2)

The Wood Walk A copy of the poem in the hand of Caroline Austen, following the poem on Anna's wedding day (p. 000), is given the title 'Addressed to the same Sister – married -- supposed to be written by the Genius of the Wood walk at Steventon' (HRO 23M93/86/5/1).

Live all his years of Childhood oer again Two years earlier James Austen had

had similar thoughts about his son's feelings when in future years he would return to Steventon:

You'll love each feature to retrace
Of this still interesting place:
This terrace, where you often stood,
And caught from yonder fading wood
The mellow note of distant hound,
Or the horn's hoarse but cheerful sound.
The little elm encircled mead,
Where whilome for your favourite steed
You marked a course, & on his back
Still made him keep the circling track:
The barn, where many a rainy day
You with your sister spent in play:
The woodwalk, where in finer weather
Beneath the shade you sat together;
All these, & every object near,
Will to your eyes more fair appear
Than any scenes you since have known:
And haply, with a sigh you'll own,
That in life's ever varying round,
Joys pure as these you have not found.

(James Austen, 'To Edward On planting a lime tree on the terrace in the meadow before the house. ---January 1813.' *The Complete Poems of James Austen*, p. 55)

That human happiness is but a dream A copy of the poem in the hand of Caroline Austen (in HRO 23M93/86/5/1) omits the last eight lines and substitutes:

Anna! the summer which at home I past,
Eer yet a different lot on each was cast;
I was no Wykamist, nor thou a wife --
I count the happiest of my happy life --
Witness ye walks, by summer evening's shade
When laughing, talking, arm in arm we strayed;
Witness ye lanes, through which we strolled along --
Ye hills, which echoed to my Anna's song --
Witness the pleasure which the memory gives --
That man has few such blessings while he lives –

At the end she adds 'The remainder is lost'.

45 TO CAROLINE ON HER BIRTHDAY Source: autograph MS 'Fugitive Pieces 2nd'. Caroline Mary Craven Austen, third child of the Revd James Austen, was born at Steventon on 18 June 1805 and this birthday poem was written in 1815, following an illness that she had suffered during the previous month. Four years earlier her father had written a poem for her sixth birthday (see *The Complete Poems of James Austen,* p. 37).

Sickness e'en may visit you 'In the May of this year I had an illness such as was then called bilious fever. Soon after I recovered, we went to spend a week at Eversley [Hants]. Mr Debary was the clergyman there, and his sisters lIved with him.... The Sunday which we passed there, and it was a very hot one, was the 18th June -- the decisive day of the Battle of Waterloo. I do not remember how soon afterwards it was, that the news of the victory reached England.' (Caroline Austen, *Reminiscences,* p. 46)

All the Mothers graces mild Again, a very different view of Mary Lloyd from Jane Austen's (see note above, p. 103).

47 ON THE DEFEAT OF BUONAPARTE AT WATERLOO Source: autograph MS 'Fugitive Pieces'. In a letter to his father of 25 July 1815 JEAL wrote: 'I like your verses on Polyxena [see below, p. 116]; we have been doing some English lines on the late victory over Buonaparte. The Dr. [Henry Gabell, Headmaster of Winchester College] said that one passage was very well written indeed.' (TS HRO 23M93/86/4/1 f. 2) JEAL's violent denunciation of Napoleon as a tyrant guilty of the spilling of much blood who will be called to account for his crimes by 'the latest judge of all' accords with Southey's view of a man with a 'soul ... incarnadined' committing 'acts of perfidy, midnight murder, usurpation, and remorseless tyranny, which have consigned his name to universal execration, now and forever' *(Life of Nelson,* 1813). Yet Jane Austen copied out Byron's sympathetic poem 'Farewell to the Land', written in the character of Napoleon, which was published in the radical weekly *The Examiner* of 30 July 1815, which suggests that she may not have regarded him with quite as much horror as her nephew did. Brian Southam considers the question of her attitude to Napoleon in 'Was Jane Austen a Bonapartist?', Jane Austen Society *Collected Reports* vol. V, 1996-2000, pp. 312-20.

Gallia See note above, p. 106.

Bourbons just command The Bourbons ruled France from 1589 (Henry IV) to 1793 (Louis XVI) and were restored in April 1814 when, on the fall of Napoleon, Louis XVIII became king; expelled during Napoleon's return (the 'hundred days'), he returned after Waterloo.

Albions England's.

thy anxious King forsake Presumably Louis XVI, guillotined in the Revolution.

Welsley's Head Arthur Wellesley, 1st Duke of Wellington. In this poem he receives full praise from JEAL (see note on Blücher, below).

49 THE HEROES Source: autograph MS 'Fugitive Pieces'. This poem, presumably dating from the summer of 1815 after the defeat of Napoleon at Waterloo on 18 June, stresses the importance of expressing gratitude to those returning from the war; in *Persuasion* the theme was to be treated with searing irony in Sir Walter Elliot's attitude to Naval officers.

Pamassus's quire The nine Muses, who dwelt at Helicon, a part of Mount Parnassus. The reference is consistent with the title, which itself invokes a classical idea.

Nayids Naiads (water-nymphs).

Blucher Gebhard Leberecht von Blücher, the Prussian field marshal, who played a crucial part in the allied victory. It is interesting that it is he, rather than Wellington, whom JEAL singles out as worthy of particular mention.

50 EPITAPH ON OLD JUSTICE Source: autograph MS 'Fugitive Pieces'. Ostensibly a lament on the putting down of a hound (a common enough occurrence in a pack of foxhounds), the poem makes play with the coincidence of the animal's name, Justice, and the fact that it could no longer work because of increasing blindness; JEAL subsequently extends this into a series of puns on the names of other hounds.

Georges ear George Hickson was formerly whipper-in of the Vine Hunt; when he succeeded to the eminent position of huntsman he never, as JEAL put it, 'attained to the dignity of a surname, but was still called "George" (J.E. Austen-Leigh, *Recollections of the Early Days of the Vine Hunt*, p. 54).

cast Search.

Blucher An interesting addition to the traditional range of names given to hounds (see note above).

52 ULISSES ANNOUNCES TO HECUBA THAT THE MANES OF ACHILLES DEMAND THE DEATH OF POLIXENA Source: autograph MS 'Fugitive Pieces 2nd'. A poem with this title exists in an MS containing poetry by James Austen (HRO 23M93/60/3/1) and I included it in *The Complete Poems of James Austen* (pp. 56-9). James sent a copy to his son (see note above, p. 115), and it may well have suggested to JEAL that he might write his own version. It is reasonable to assume that JEAL completed his, even though for some reason he copied only the opening lines into his album. The source of the story, which was treated by among others Euripides, Seneca, Ovid and Quintus of Smyrna, is the Epic Cycle. After the fall of Troy, Achilles, requiring sacrifice from beyond the grave, demands that Hecuba's daughter Polyxena should be killed.

Manes Shades of the dead.

that stately Mein After Ulysses has spoken to her in James Austen's poem, she displays a 'wild disordered mien'.

[thou] MS: though.

53 TO MAMMA Source: autograph MS 'Fugitive Pieces 2nd'. Though JEAL implies that he has not previously written a poem for his mother, in fact he had (see p. 9 and note above, p. 103); if he thought the earlier one unsatisfactory, it is presumably part of the joke that now he can manage nothing more than an epigram.

54 MOSES Source: MS in album, watermark 1873, HRO 23M93/86/5/1. The poem is based on the account in Exodus XVII of Moses striking the rock (a slightly different version is found in Numbers XX), though it considerably amplifies the details given there. From the challenge to the authority of Moses -- and of God -- in the opening command (subsequently repeated several times to considerable rhetorical effect) to the gushing of water from the rock and its immediate effect on the Children of Israel, JEAL responds excitedly to the drama of the events. The grievances of the Israelites and their regret at having left Egypt, Moses' rebuke and his prayer, and the working of the miracle, are all given energy and pace; and the handling of the heroic couplet finds JEAL at his most assured.

Commoners The hall in Winchester College for those pupils who were not scholars.

paschal lamb See Exodus XII.

the land of Ham Egypt. The name is used in the later Psalms.

Safe from the fury of the Heavenly King A telling irony: the Israelites have forgotten the terrible punishment visited on the Egyptians in the killing of the firstborn.

murmured The word 'murmur' recurs frequently in these passages of Exodus.

in the plains of Sin JEAL conflates the 'murmurs' of the Israelites here: while they were in the wilderness of Sin they complained of hunger; the demand for water occurs at Rephidim (see Exodus XVII. 1). The account in Numbers XX places the event in the Wilderness of Zin, but the rock is unnamed, since Zin is a long way from Horeb.

Provoked their mightier God The impiety is marked by a well-placed Alexandrine.

They eyed each stone 'And Moses cried unto the LORD, saying, What shall I do unto this people? they be almost ready to stone me.' (Exodus XVII. 4)

As bursts refulgent The syntax here seems to be muddled.

"Ungrateful minions!..." No speech to the Israelites is given in either of the Biblical passages. *your dread passage through the opening deep* See Exodus XIV. 21-29.

the pillar of the Lord 'And the LORD went before them by day in a pillar of a cloud, to lead them the way; and by night in a pillar of fire to give them light; to go by day and night: He took not away the pillar of the cloud by day, nor the pillar of fire by night, from the people.' (Exodus XIII. 21-22)

Marah Where God shows Moses a tree which he casts into the water to make it drinkable (see Exodus XV. 23-35).

Manna See Exodus XVI. 13 ff.

Prometheus As a punishment for stealing fire from heaven and giving it to men Prometheus was bound to Mount Caucasus, where an eagle (or a vulture) ate his liver every day, the organ being renewed each night. The story is the theme of Aeschylus's tragedy *Prometheus Bound.*

There Moses stood The strikingly imagined details of the scene are JEAL's: in Exodus XVII God commands Moses to strike the rock and the action is described in one brief sentence: 'And Moses did so in the sight of the elders of Israel.'

Exulting nature gladdened This proto-Romantic touch is far removed from the world of the Old Testament.

58 TO THE MEMORY OF MISS JANE AUSTEN Source: autograph MS in the collection of David Gilson Esq. On 10 December 1934 Richard Arthur Austen-Leigh wrote to R.W. Chapman about this poem, 'I am glad you are not thinking of printing it, for I think it must be admitted that the sentiments are superior to the poetry', and it is hard not to disagree with this view. Although it has much in common with James Austen's tribute (*The Complete Poems of James Austen*, p. 86), JEAL's language lacks his father's aspirations to verbal grandeur and he is too ready to resort to the stock vocabulary of 18th-century mourning. The hymnlike stanza form is also unfortunate, though it must be admitted that James's tripping octosyllabic couplets are hardly more

118

appropriate; Collins's Ode on the death of James Thomson (1749), which would have been known to both of them, is more satisfactory in employing alternately rhymed octosyllabic lines that hold back the pace:

> In yonder Grave a DRUID lies
> Where slowly winds the stealing Wave!
> The Year's best Sweets shall duteous rise
> To deck it's POET's sylvan Grave!

Venta's consecrated Pile Winchester Cathedral. Cf. the opening of James Austen's poem:

> Venta! within thy sacred fane
> Rests many a chief, in battle slain,
> And many a Statesman great & wise
> Beneath thy hallowed pavement lies:
> Tracing thy venerable pile,
> Thy Gothic choir and Pillared Aisle;
> Frequent we tread the vaulted grave
> Where sleep the learned & the Brave.

The Warton whom she loved Not the poet Thomas Warton, Professor of Poetry and subsequently Camden Professor of Ancient History at Oxford, and Poet Laureate, but his elder brother Joseph (1722-1800), who became headmaster of Winchester College and was best known as a critic. His 'Ode to Fancy' (1746) influenced her youthful 'Ode to Pity' (see *Jane Austen: Collected Poems and verse of the Austen Family,* p. 78). Flaxman's monument to him is in the south aisle of the cathedral.

Wyckham William of Wykeham (c. 1323-1404), Chancellor of England and founder of New College, Oxford and Winchester College, as Bishop of Winchester remodelled the original Norman nave of the cathedral. Cf. James Austen:

> ...honoured Wickham lies reclined
> In Gothic tracery enshrined.

(11. 15-16)

Right justly wert thou laid Possible reasons for Jane Austen's burial in the Cathedral have often been discussed. Michael Wheeler, in *Jane Austen and Winchester Cathedral* (Winchester, 2003), points out that, while the fact that she died in the parish of St Swithun entitled her to be buried in the Cathedral precinct, for her to be buried inside the Cathedral she and her family must have had strong connections in the Close; and he goes on to suggest that Henry Austen, who made the funeral arrangements, may have been supported in his request to the Dean (himself a friend of the Chutes of the Vyne) by Mrs Elizabeth Heathcote. Yet JEAL seems quite clear in the poem that her 'Genius', as well as her 'Piety' merited the place; though the reference to possible exclusion may imply that there had been some difficulties in obtaining the necessary permission.

If purest Taste, if brightest Mind Cf. Jane Austen, 'To the Memory of Mrs. Lefroy':

> I listen -- 'tis not sound alone -- 'tis sense,
> 'Tis Genius, Taste, & Tenderness of Soul.
> 'Tis genuine warmth of heart without pretence
> And purity of Mind that crowns the whole.
>> (*Jane Austen: Collected Poems and verse of the Austen Family,* p. 9)

The purple Flowret of the Vale The violet.

from Cowper's Tomb In his 'Biographical Notice' to *Northanger Abbey* and *Persuasion* Henry Austen says that Jane Austen's 'favourite moral writers were Johnson in prose, and Cowper in verse'. William Cowper (1731-1800) published *Poems* in 1782, and the volume included his eight satires, though JEAL is no doubt referring to the poet's work more generally.

without his Horn Satyrs were portrayed by the Romans with goat's ears and budding horns.

One half-repining Tear Cf. James Austen:

> ...when upon a Sister's bier
> Her brothers dropt the bitter tear.
>> (11. 23-4)

great change shall be '... the dead shall be raised incorruptible, and we shall be changed.' (1 Corinthians XV. 52)

The blood that saved a Magdalen's Soul The thought is clear enough: 'If it were possible for the soul to escape tainting by its earthly embodiment, yours would be pure; but since it is not, even you will be redeemed.' But the comparison with Mary Magdalen is hardly apt.

62 LETTER TO MRS. B. LEFROY. WYARDS AFTER A BASINGSTOKE BALL

Source: autograph MS sent to Caroline Austen, HRO 23M93/66/2; a copy in her hand (HRO 23M93/86/5/1) gives both the title and the date, 11 October 1818. JEAL prefaces the verse: 'In reply to the following Passage in Anna's letter to me "I hope you had a pleasant Ball -- I sh^d. like to hear about it, who you danced with, wether you wore a blue coat or a black one, how many cups of Tea you drank, & wether you were agreable or not. But of all things I hope you did not dance with Miss Standen."' This playful response to a request from Anna for information about a ball at Basingstoke is similar to an earlier letter, also in verse, by his grandmother, Mrs George Austen, in which she had listed, for the benefit of either Jane or Cassandra, the names of all those who attended a Basingstoke ball in November 1799 (see *Jane Austen: Collected Poems and verse of the Austen Family*, p. 29); JEAL confines himself for the most part to naming his dancing partners – or in the case of Miss Standen a rejected one. He makes amusing use of heraldic terms to describe his appearance, and the easy grace of his endearing mock immodesty in the last two lines shows why he was such a favourite with the family.

Wyards The farmhouse a mile to the north of Chawton where Anna and Ben Lefroy had been living since 1815.

a Basingstoke Ball Balls were held at the Town Hall and the Austens were regular attenders (see Robin Vick, 'The Basingstoke Assemblies', *Collected Reports* vol. IV, p. 304).

Wether sable or vert China tea -- tea was not imported from India until 1839 -- was drunk both black and green (unfermented); that JEAL could not tell which he was drinking says something for the quantity of sugar and cream he must have put in!

Mrs. Blackstone Margaret Blackstone (1768-1841), eldest sister of Harris Bigg-Wither of Manydown Park, Wootton St Lawrence, Hants., and widow of the vicar of Andover. In a letter to Anna three years later, 20 December 1821 (TS HRO 23M93/86/4/1 f.8), after describing one ball at Alresford, he looks forward to another, at Basingstoke, on 3 January and informs her: 'I am to be at Worting with Mrs. Blackstone for it; so I must of course begin with her daughter.'

Caroline Wiggett Adopted daughter of the Chutes of The Vyne (1799-187?).

Margaret Blackstone Daughter of Mrs Blackstone, above. Margaret, Caroline, William Heathcote and JEAL were all close friends (see Robert Heathcote Lawrence, 'Jane Austen at Manydown', *Collected Reports* vol. V, pp. 347-50).

Boulanger The country dance is thus spelt in *P&P* (p. 13); when describing the dancing at Goodnestone in September 1796, Jane Austen spells it Boulangeries (*L*, p. 8); but as Deirdre Le Faye points out (*L*, p. 356), it should be Boulangères.

Mʳ. Lane If this is the Mr Edward Lane, of Worting, a relation of the Bigg-Withers, who attended the ball described by Mrs Austen (see above), he may have been large: she refers to him as 'great Squire Lane'.

Mr. Augustus Hare Augustus Hare (1792-1834), the clergyman and author, had in 1818 just returned from Italy to take up an appointment as tutor at New Collge, Oxford. He was the nephew of Lady Jones of Worting House, near Basingstoke.

64 TO THE MEMORY OF THE REVD JAMES AUSTEN Source: autograph MS, HRO 23M93/86/5/3. James Austen died in 1819, after many years of failing health. Caroline wrote: 'It was about a week before his death that he became aware he was sinking fast. My brother came from Oxford. On 13th December 1819 my father breathed his last, at half-past eleven at night. On Saturday the 18th he was buried in Steventon churchyard; the grave being made on the spot he had long before chosen for his resting-place. The funeral was attended by my brother and our four uncles.' (*Reminiscences*, p. 56) On the reverse of the MS, in the hand of JEAL: 'To the Memory of the Revd James Austen, / many years Minister of this Parish, / who died Dec^{er}. 13. 1819 / Aged – This Monument is erected by his Children / This paper contains the true copy of the intended monument for my Father, both in prose & verse – J.E. Austen.' There are various designs for the stone and, upside down in pencil (presumably added later by Emma Austen-Leigh), 'Dearest Edwards lines engraved on his Father's Monument in Steventon Church Yard'. In fact the wording on the monument in St Nicholas, Steventon (on the chancel wall, not on the gravestone in the churchyard) differs considerably from that in the MS and the verse was extensively rewritten. The inscription reads:

TO THE MEMORY OF
THE REVD. JAMES AUSTEN
WHO SUCCEEDED HIS FATHER THE REVD. GEORGE AUSTEN
AS RECTOR OF THIS PARISH
AND DIED DEC 13TH. 1819 AGED 53 YEARS,
THIS MONUMENT AND THE STONE WHICH COVERS
HIS GRAVE IN THE CHURCHYARD
WERE ERECTED BY HIS WIDOW AND CHILDREN

The verse was finally inscribed as follows:

THERE MIDST THE FLOCK HIS FOND ATTENTION FED,
THE VILLAGE PASTOR RESTS HIS WEARY HEAD.
TILL CALLED TO JOIN, FROM SIN AND SUFFERING FREED,
THAT HEAVENLY FLOCK WHICH CHRIST HIMSELF SHALL FEED.
FOR LONG AND WELL HE BORE THE CHASTENING ROD,
LONG MARKED FOR DEATH THE VALE OF LIFE HE TROD.
FOR TALENTS HONOURED, THOUGH TO FEW DISPLAYED,
AND VIRTUES BRIGHTENING THROUGH DEJECTIONS SHADE,
SIMPLE YET WISE MOST FREE FROM GUILE OR PRIDE,
HE DAILY LIVED TO GOD, AND DAILY DIED.

BEST EARLIEST FRIEND; FOR THEE WHOSE CARES ARE O'ER
DEAR AS THY PRESENCE WAS, WE GRIEVE NO MORE.
WELL TAUGHT BY THEE, OUR HEARTS CAN HEAVENWARD RISE,
WE DARE NO SORROW, WHERE A CHRISTIAN DIES.

The Lord hath let his Servant part in peace A reference to the Nunc dimittis (Luke II. 29), which begins 'Lord, now lettest thou thy servant depart in peace', and is sung at Evening Prayer (*BCP*).

65 LINES TO DYCE WRITTEN 1821 Source: autograph MS 'Fugitive Pieces 2nd'. The title is given only in the list of Contents. With its structure of two quatrains and a six-line stanza repeated only once, the poem feels incomplete -- but perhaps JEAL's Greek studies won the day after all. Alexander Dyce (1798-1869) was a contemporary of JEAL's at Exeter College, Oxford (BA 1819, ordained 1823); subsequently he became a distinguished scholar and editor, producing editions of, among others, Collins, Peele, Webster, Marlowe, Pope, Shakespeare, Middleton, Skelton and Ford. In 1821 he published his *Select Translations from the Greek of Quintus Smyrnaeus*, which was greeted by this squib from his friend. They were close at Oxford and were still corresponding in 1828, when Dyce congratulated JEAL on his forthcoming marriage, while warning him in a P.S., 'Don't expect an Epithalamium from me' (HRO 23M93/86/3b - 55). But the friendship became difficult to sustain; JEAL's daughter Mary Augusta Austen-Leigh wrote of Dyce: 'Though well known to the world as the great authority on Shakespeare, he became such a recluse that before long he gave up visiting even his intimate friends, and I have heard our mother say that early in their married life our father repeatedly but vainly tried to induce him to come to them, till at last he gave it up in despair. These old friends, however, also met once in later life, when Mr. Dyce was persuaded to come for a few hours from London to Bray Vicarage. We thought him a charming old man with a fine face and gentle, dignified manners. He did not live to repeat the visit.' (*James Edward Austen Leigh: A memoir*, p. 9) The next poem in 'Fugitive Pieces 2nd' is a 'Letter to Dyce at Oxford written from Donnington Cottage, Oct^{er}. 1821' in Latin (omitted).

Ω Δίχε, – ω φιλόλογε O Dyce, – O lover of literature.

Quintus Calaber Quintus Smyrnaeus, the Greek epic poet writing in the latter part of the 4th cent. AD. He was the author of the *Posthomerica*, a poem in 14 books taking up the tale of Troy at the point where the *Iliad* breaks off; the MS was discovered in Calabria, hence his sobriquet.

boughs of birchen schoolmasters' canes.

some generous sons of song Among them Dyce. In fact his translation was the first ever to be published, as he himself noted in his preface. The four sections he included were 'The Valour and Death of Penthesilea', 'Arrival of Memnon at Troy; his Valiant Deeds and Death', 'The Death of Achilles' and 'The Shield and Helmet of Achilles'. Dyce observed that 'Verbosity being the prevailing fault of Quintus', he had 'shortened ... several of the speeches and descriptions', modestly adding 'I have made use of blank verse in preference to rhyme ... I expect, therefore, to be told by the admirers of Pope's Homer that my lines are intolerably prosaic'.

67 A LETTER FROM AN UNDERGRADUATE TO HIS FRIEND, DESCRIPTIVE OF THE LATE COMMEMORATION Source: MS HRO 23M93/86/5/4, which is missing its last page; the final 27 lines are supplied from a copy in the hand of Caroline Austen, HRO 23M93/86/5/1 (with variants), in which the title is given as 'To Mrs. B. Lefroy -- Wyards' with an indecipherable date in October 1818 followed by 'But probably the summer of 1818 Possibly 1817. From Oxford.' Anna was undoubtedly the recipient of the poem. The ceremony over which JEAL casts a somewhat satirical eye is the annual Encaenia, a meeting of Convocation presided over by the Chancellor, which in JEAL's time was held in July, on a Wednesday three weeks from the beginning of what was then Oxford's fourth term, and which marked the climax of the academic year. The week was known as the Commemoration, from the Creweian Oration in commemoration of the benefactors to the University which precedes the conferring of honorary degrees and the recitation of prize compositions. Finding himself in languid mood at the end of the term, JEAL begins his poem with a repudiation of the heroic (i.e. iambic) line and, invoking his muse, presents a very unclassical picture of her sipping tea with her sister muses as they laugh at any young man foolish enough to take the trouble to write poetry. After descriptions of the arrival in Oxford of large numbers of visitors for the occasion -- including women -- and the procession and ceremony itself, he ends with an ironic glimpse of another poet, the winner of the Newdigate Prize reading his verse, which at that time was to be 'in recommendation of the study of the ancient Greek and Roman remains of Architecture, Sculpture and Painting' and did have to be in heroic couplets. The line numbers are given in the MS.

wast Waste: in this sense, pass or spend.

Balls Traditionally held during the week of Commemoration.

Landauletts and Curricles A landaulette was a closed four-wheeled carriage, a curricle a light two-wheeled gig generally for two horses (as opposed to the one-horse gig that John Thorpe bought from 'a Christchurch man' on Magdalen Bridge -- see *NA*, p. 46).

Helicon The home of the Muses (see n. above, p. 116).

The Eye in a fine Phrensy rolling A Midsummer Nights Dream, V.i. 1. 12.

Bohea Low quality black tea.

Castalia A fountain of Parnassus sacred to the Muses.

leading Strings With which children learning to walk were held up.

Barouch Landaus The barouche-landau was a comparatively new vehicle when Mr Suckling acquired his *(E,* p. 274), having first appeared in 1804 (see *MP* p. 564).

Provost's Gothic door The heads of some colleges are called provosts.

Pluto In Roman myth the ruler of the underworld.

shewn HRO 23M93/86/5/1: looked.

Gownsmen All members of the university entitled to wear gowns.

Academics Academic dress.

Tufts Gold tassels attached to mortar-boards worn by the sons of noblemen.

Silk gowns Doctors' gowns have silk facings.

Commoners Members of a college who are not 'on the foundation' (i.e. the Master, Fellows and scholars); Caroline Austen describes the trouble that JEAL and his mother went to in order to prove his entitlement to a Craven Scholarship in *Reminiscences,* pp. 49-50.

Servitors Undergraduates who waited on Fellows or other wealthier undergraduates in return for reduced fees.

Scout College servant (until recently exclusively male).

Parkers Prints Not Parker's, on the corner of Broad Street and Turl Street, which was then Fletcher and Hanwell, but the bookshop at 88 High Street established by Dr Johnson's friend Sackville Parker.

Spier's Stationery and fancy goods shop.

A Pincoushin HRO 23M93/86/5/1: An Allumette (i.e. a match).

A Woodstock glove Glovemaking was the principal industry of the town of Woodstock, Oxon.

Theatre The Sheldonian Theatre in Broad Street was Wren's first architectural work; Encaenia and other degree ceremonies are held there.

Drury The large and lavish Drury Lane Theatre in London. Jane Austen saw Edmund Kean as Shylock there in 1814.

scarlet Hoods worn by holders of all doctorates at Oxford, except that in Music, are of scarlet cloth.

The outside of the platter's clean Both MSS append a note, only fully readable in 23M93/86/5/1: 'For these suspicions & aspersions vide Oxford Spy, which you have not got to look at.'

Beadles Four Bedels, carrying staves, still act as attendants to the Vice-Chancellor at the various ceremonies of the University. The post of Esquire Bedel was abolished in 1856.

mighty Man The Vice-Chancellor, who held office for four (not three) years. In

JEAL's time at Oxford the Vice-Chancellors were Thomas Lee, DD, President of Trinity (1814-18) and Frodsham Hodson, DD, Principal of Brasenose (1818-20).

Proctors The two disciplinary officers of the University, elected annually; their full black gowns have sleeves of royal-blue velvet.

Benefactors In 23M93/86/5/1 the lines are given thus:

> While Benefactors, long forgotten
> Whose memory like their bones, grows rotten

There is also a note: 'Before the successful compositions are repeated, a Latin Oration is spoken by the Public Orator, in praise of Benefactors to the University.'

The Classic Bard of There is a blank in the MS, and the lines are omitted from 23M93/86/5/1. Possibly a reference to John Dyer, author of the poem *Grongar Hill* (1726), which had an influence on the poetry of James Austen and is referred to by him in his poem 'Selbourne Hanger' *(The Complete Poems of James Austen*, p. 46); but it is not easy to see the connection with Oxford.

Pellesse Pelisse, a long mantle with sleeves or armholes, worn by women.

Spencer A short jacket.

[gorgeous] MS: georgious. The line has been omitted in 23M93/86/5/1.

[Though] The MS has 'Thou'; the 4th word of the line is missing.

73 'MIRROR OF LIFE' Source: Mary Augusta Austen-Leigh, *J.E. Austen Leigh: A memoir* (privately printed, 1911), p. 24. Written while he was living with his mother and younger sister in a house in the Donnington Road at Speen, near Newbury, this is one of JEAL's most successful poems. The details of already half-forgotten events contained in the pages of a pocket book discarded at the end of the year lead him to muse on the necessarily trivial nature of our daily life; but possible criticism from an imaginary reader of the diary is dismissed with a tolerant recognition of the general frailty of human nature. The final two lines are particularly effective.

monumental Serving as a memorial.

74 LINES ACCOMPANYING A PEARL PIN, ADDRESSED TO WILLIAM HEATHCOTE ON FRIDAY MAY 17ᵀᴴ: 1822. ON WHICH DAY HE CAME OF AGE. Source: autograph MS 'Fugitive Pieces 2nd'. Writing verses to accompany gifts was a habit with the Austen family (as no doubt with many others); JEAL himself wrote one to go with a gift of a knife to his father (see above, p. 8) and Jane Austen wrote poems to accompany handkerchiefs and a little needlework bag. JEAL views his earlier versifying as an activity of youth, and is perhaps hinting that he does not feel he has the talent to continue it into adult life. Nevertheless, the plant metaphor at the end of the poem, strengthened by the addition of an extra line in the final verse, seems very successful.

William Heathcote See note above, p. 110.

Winchester William Heathcote was at this time living with his mother and his aunt, Alethea Bigg, in a house in the Cathedral close at Winchester.

76 PROLOGUE TO THE SULTAN Source: MS in the hand of Caroline Austen HR023M93/66/3/1. JEAL is here following his father in providing a prologue and epilogue for the private performance of a play, in this case Isaac Bickerstaffe's two-act comedy of 1775.

Ashington Parsonage In the village of Ashington, between Horsham and Worthing in Sussex, where the Revd Henry Warren (1772-1845), son of the physician to George IV and a nephew of the Bishop of Bangor, was rector; he was a cousin of JEAL's friend the Revd Henry William Majendie, vicar of Speen. The date of the performance was 18 June 1823.

Elmira See below.

Ismena See below.

so MS: 'too' cancelled.

Osmyn The keeper of the harem.

77 AN EPILOGUE TO THE SULTAN Source: autograph MS 'Fugitive Pieces 2nd'. There is an epilogue to *The Sultan* among the prologues and epilogues that James Austen wrote for performances at Steventon rectory between 1782 and 1789; spoken by Roxalana, the lively English heroine who sees off the whole of the Sultan's harem to become sole empress, it wittily celebrates the tactics of female dominance, and is one of his most amusing poems (*The Complete Poems of James Austen*, p. 27). By contrast, JEAL's epilogue is written for the Sultan and gallantly expresses his sense of decline from being 'the mightiest' on stage to 'the lowliest' when the curtain descends, since he is the only male performer.

Ashington See above.

three *tails* Perhaps referring to two other short plays or scenes performed with *The Sultan*.

three wives The empress Elmira, the slave girl Ismena and the doughty Roxalana.

The rebel Osmyn He was played in this performance by a woman.

with seeming sway The acknowledgment of *apparent* male dominance in marriage is noteworthy and is emphasised by an alexandrine.

Miss Warren The eldest of Henry Warren's twelve children was Eliza, b. 1800.

79 LINES WRITTEN AT BEAR HILL COTTAGE, BERKSHIRE Source: autograph MS 'Fugitive Pieces 2nd'. Bear Hill Cottage, subsequently Bear Hill Villa, was close to Scarlets, the home of JEAL's great-aunt, Mrs Leigh-Perrot, near Wargrave, Berks. It was owned by the Fonnereau family; Mr Fonnereau was a friend of Mrs Leigh-Perrot, and following her husband's death he offered to be named a trustee of the Scarlets estate jointly with James Austen, who was in declining health. She subsequently bought Bear Hill Cottage with other properties and added them to the Scarlets estate, which JEAL inherited at her death in 1837. In this poem he pays an elaborate tribute to the pleasantness of the house and its occupants in terms of an extended and exotic analogy.

81 ON A RUN FROM MILK HILL Source: autograph MS 'Fugitive Pieces 2nd'. In a notebook recording his hunting activities between 1820 and 1825 (HRO 23M93/86/7/2), JEAL included annual lists of the Vine hounds; that for 1822-23 has Gamester added and crossed through in 1822, suggesting he lasted only one season, and possibly giving a date for the poem (though oddly Precious, Latimer, and Lavish fail to appear in any of the lists). The amount of time that JEAL devoted to hunting at this time can be seen from a note for the 1823-4 season:

I hunted, this year, 60 times –

	times		foxes
with Chute	20	killed	13
Warde	21	killed	7
Cope	6	killed	3
Villebois	6	killed	1
Codrington	1	killed	0
	60		24

	times
Rode Skeleton	39
Nutley	5
May	11
Mounted by Mr. Fowle	2
C. Craven	2
Johnson	1
	60

In this lively, but unfortunately incomplete, account of a run with the Vine Hunt, the rhythm, in galloping anapaests, conveys the excitement of the chase.

Milk hill Milk hill copse, between Litchfield and Whitchurch, Hants.

Harmsworth At Old Alresford, between Winchester and Alton, the location of the kennels of the Hampshire Hunt.

the hero of Heckfield Charles Shaw-Lefevre of Heckfield Place near Basingstoke, MP for Reading, acquired a great deal of land, a process continued by his son, who in 1857 was created Viscount Eversley.

Illsley West and East Illsley, Berks, in the Craven country, are a long way from Heckfield.

George George Hickson. See note above, p.000.

rattlers Very good horses.

Poleswood Paul's Wood, SE of Milk hill copse. It was a frequent meeting place for the Vine Hunt.

[Were] MS: where.

Beacon Hill SE of Highclere.

Pop George Hennessey, whipper-in with the Vine, and subsequently huntsman to Mr Charles Craven of the East Sussex. 'A good-humoured broad-shouldered fellow known to us only by the nickname of Pop, which he had inherited from his father, a veteran post-boy at Overton' (James Edward Austen-Leigh, *Recollections of the Early Days of the Vine Hunt*, p. 60).

groom Squire Presumably William Chute.

elft Tangled.

Croakers Dismal, pessimistic speakers.

That the farther they rode, they The line may have been completed by 'got farther behind'.

83 PROLOGUE SPOKEN BY EDWARD IN THE CHARACTER OF 'SCRUB OF THE COMPANY,' Source: Mary Augusta Austen-Leigh, *J.E. Austen Leigh*, pp. 156-57. Recalling in both rhythm and spirit James Austen's 'Epilogue to the Sultan' *(The Complete Poems of James Austen*, p. 26), JEAL's theatrical prologue lacks something of his father's comic flair -- though there are one or two good lines and it ends amusingly on a note of gleeful ungenerosity. JEAL's daughter provides the background to the poem: 'An entertainment on a large scale was given at Suttons [in Essex] in 1851, where our cousin, Sir Charles Smith, and his sisters were then established. On September 2 our parents with Amy [Emma, JEAL's eldest daughter] and four sons, Julia and Fanny Lefroy [JEAL's nieces], and two servants, went together to Suttons for ten days, when a dramatic entertainment, followed by a dance, was given to the neighbourhood. The dining-room was the ballroom, and through this the guests were ushered into the reception (the octagon) room, and thence into the drawing-room, arranged as a theatre at its farther end, so that the performers had access through the door on that side to the staircase and to their own rooms above. The supper and tea were in the hall and the study. A charade, "Testy Money," [Testimony] was acted. *1st* Scene.---From "The Rivals." (Many scenes, in which Sir Anthony Absolute appears, being given.) *2nd* Scene.---From "Nicholas Nickleby" (Peg Sliderskew and Arthur Gride). *Last Scene.*---Trial Scene in "Pickwick." It was followed by "Box and Cox." On the morning of the performance our father, when taking a solitary ride to Ongar, composed a prologue which Edward learnt and repeated in the evening.' (Mary Augusta Austen-Leigh, *.JE. Austen-Leigh,* pp. 155-56) She also quotes (p. 250) an epilogue, written by JEAL's eldest son, Cholmeley, and spoken in the character of Bob Acres in *The Rivals;* it begins 'Odds, whips, wheels and linchpins! Just up from the West / With my hair and my person not properly drest' and strongly recalls an epilogue to the same play by James Austen (*The Complete Poems of James Austen,* p. 11). In her diary JEAL's wife noted that there were 'between 50 & 60 persons present' (HRO 23M93/87/1/36).

Edward Edward Compton Austen-Leigh (1839-1916), seventh of JEAL's ten children.

a 'Sell." A disappointment.

safe Sure.

lubberly Lazy, stupid.

Mr. Winkle Mr Pickwick's friend in Dickens's *Pickwick Papers.*

85 ŒNIGMA WRITTEN AT CHAWTON IN THE SUMMER 1820 (YE NYMPHS OF CHAWTON) Source: autograph MS 'Fugitive Pieces 2nd'.

[Solution: Spadille] The use of the heroic couplet, the terming of the ladies 'Nymphs' and above all the representation of the game of ombre as a scene of battle all strongly recall Pope's *The Rape of the Lock.*

Œnigma 'Charade' cancelled. An enigma is a riddle containing one or more meanings of a word or phrase, whereas in a charade the syllables have to be solved separately before the full word is found.

Nymphs of Chawton JEAL was visiting his grandmother and aunts Cassandra Austen and Martha Lloyd at Chawton Cottage.

the level green The green baize covering of a card table; the pun of course is on 'sporting' on e.g. a village 'green'.

three strong brethren In the game of ombre, and in its four-handed derivative quadrille, there are three 'matadores', cards which have special powers; they are, in descending rank, Spadille, the Ace of Spades, Manille, the nominally lowest trump (Two if black, Seven if red) and Basto, the Ace of Clubs.

lines engraved around my front From 1718 the Ace of Spades had been stamped to show that duty had been paid on the pack, but from 1765 the card was printed by the tax office with an elaborate design. In 1820 the tax on a pack of playing cards was 2*s.* 6*d.*

Prince Sovereign (George IV had succeeded to the throne in January 1820).

86 ENIGMA Source: Gilson MS. [Solution: Hope] The perpetual endurance and universal benefit of hope are ended only when they are no longer needed; with wonderful reassurance, the death of hope, simultaneous with the death of the individual, occurs only at the moment of its dissolution into 'actual bliss'. Though written in the form of a puzzle, the poem is one of the most serious JEAL wrote; in its use of deft wordplay to reinforce a religious theme it recalls the poetry of George Herbert.

What loves the anchor The anchor is a Christian symbol of hope, deriving from Hebrews VI. 19, 'Which *hope* we have as an anchor of the soul, both sure and stedfast'.

Like charity all griefs would cure In this and the subsequent line JEAL appears to view hope as being equal to charity, whereas I Corinthians XIII. 13 has: 'And now abideth faith, hope, charity, these three; but the greatest of these is charity.'

Like charity can much endure I Corinthians XIII. 4: 'Charity suffereth long, *and* is kind'.

87 'MY 1ST. IS OFT DONE' Source: Gilson MS. [Solution: Breakfast]

87 'MY 1ST. IS OF NATURE' Source: Gilson MS. [Solution: ?Waterglass]

88 'SHAKE MY 1ST.' Source: Gilson MS. [Solution: Handbill]

88 'MY FIRST, TO AID THE WORKS OF MAN' Source: autograph MS 'Fugitive Pieces 2nd', where it is given the title 'Charade'. [Solution: Windlass]

Compton JEAL was staying with his sister Anna, whose husband, the Revd Benjamin Lefroy, was curate at Compton, near Guildford, in Surrey.

89 'MY 1ˢᵀ. SHOULD BE LONG' Source: Gilson MS. [Solution: ?Pulpit]
dressed in red Possibly the cloth hanging from the reading desk in a pulpit: red is the liturgical colour used for Whitsun and the feasts of martyrs.

90 'MY 1ˢᵀ. THO' NOW NO CHICKEN THOUGHT' Source: Gilson MS. [Solution: Henpeck]

91 'IN DAYS OF YORE' Source: *Bouts-Rimés and Noun Verses*, p.6.
double Possibly punning on the name for a small French or German coin.

91 'YOUR HOUNDS ARE MUCH TOO FRESH AND GAY' Source: *Bouts-Rimés and Noun Verses*, p. 6.
flash Move quickly.
double A sudden turn made by a hare or fox.

91 'HARK! WHERE THOSE SHADOWY WOODLANDS SLEEP' Source: *Bouts-Rimés and Noun Verses*, p. 7.
eggs and batter Eggs and butter is more usual: it is in Mrs Beeton and of course in *1 Henry IV*, I.ii, when Falstaff tells Hal that he has not so much grace 'as will serve to be prologue to an egg and butter'.

91 "OH: BETTY WHAT MAKES ME LOOK SUCH A FRIGHT?" Source: Gilson MS (but rhyme words in heading supplied from *Bouts-Rimés and Noun Verses*).

92 'HOW THICK ON THE HERALDIC PAGE' Source: Mary Augusta Austen-Leigh, *James Edward Austen Leigh: A memoir*. p. 160.
sweet Anne Page In *The Merry Wives of Windsor*.
appanage Provision made for the younger sons of kings.
Brave, fair and sage, of every age The internal rhyme points to the finality of the churchyard.

92 'THEY WHO HAVE CLIMBED THE STEEP ASCENT OF POWER' Source: *Bouts-Rimés and Noun Verses*, p. 10.

93 'I TIED UP MY LEG' Source: Gilson MS.

93 'FISHING TADPOLES FROM A DITCH' Source: Gilson MS.

93 'SOME ONE MUST PAY FOR EVERY WHISTLE' Source: *Bouts-Rimés and Noun Verses*, p.12.

Some one must pay for every whistle 'To pay for one's whistle' means to pay a high price for a whim.

Balston Dr Edward Balston, assistant master at Eton College from 1840, Headmaster 1862-68. Described by Sir William Anson as 'a man whose charm of manner endeared him to generations of pupils' and by Queen Victoria as 'the handsomest ecclesiastic in my dominions', he was remembered by Sir Leslie Stephen as 'a good scholar after the fashion of the day, and famous for his Latin verse, but ... essentially a commonplace don'. Three of JEAL's sons, Edward, Augustus and William, were at Eton during Balston's time as a master there, and Edward was subsequently appointed by him to the staff.

thistle A cane with its head carved in the shape of a thistle, appropriate for St Andrew's Day.

94 'FAINT ECHOES OF DEPARTED VERSE' Source: Gilson MS.

94 'WHAT DOES THAT FAIR GIRL'S HEART COMMEMORATE' Source: *Bouts-Rimés and Noun Verses*, p. 19.

94 'WITH VICTORIES OF EVERY KIND' Source: *Bouts-Rimés and Noun Verses*, p. 20.

Gambetta Leon Michel Gambetta (1838-82), French politician who organised the resistance in the Franco-Prussian War and in 1871 proclaimed the Third Republic.

95 "MY DEAR, I'M SURE YOUR END OF TOWN" Source: *Bouts-Rimés and Noun Verses*, p. 24.

96 'IF MERITS SHOULD BE RIGHTLY RECKONED' Source: *Bouts-Rimés and Noun Verses*, p. 28.

Sentinel In a letter of 5 May 1853 to his son Augustus, when the family were moving to Bray vicarage from Scarlets, JEAL wrote:

> Sentinel has been in a very unsettled state of mind. He was very despondent and miserable while the preparations for removing were going on at Scarlets, but last Thursday he voluntarily accompanied the ponies hither and seemed to take great interest in the place and to be in high spirits for some days. When Charles [one of Augustus's elder brothers] appeared on Saturday beyond the river and hailed a

boat, he swam the Thames to welcome him.

On Monday he accompanied Mamma and me back to Scarlets, and, when there, local attachments seemed to revive, and he could not be persuaded to return to Bray with us. However, today he came back with Favourite and Camilla and I imagine he is now settled here for life. (TS HRO 23M93/86/4/1 f. 56)

Sentinel was clearly a general favourite. When a family friend sent him a collar of knitted coral on New Year's Day 1857, Mary Augusta replied for him in verse, beginning:

> I am really most grateful, my dear Miss Teresa
> For the pains & the trouble you've taken to please a
> Poor dog like myself, in thus deigning to deck
> In so handsome a manner my scraggy old neck …

After a further 38 lines of doggerel, she allows him to sign off:

> But I fear I grow prosy, so finish my letter
> Do not laugh when you read it, I w^d. it were better.
> I see that my writing has grown rather quaky,
> And you too will find some day age makes the hand shaky
> Yet long may it be ere this happens, & oh!
> Many many a happy New Year may you know!
> May you never want friends, though you cannot have any
> More constant & warm than your faithful old Senny.
> (MS HRO 23M93/92/2)

Tweedledum and Tweedledee Though appropriated by Lewis Carroll in *Through the Looking-Glass* (1871), the names had been invented by the 18th-century poet John Byrom to satirize the rival composers Handel and Bononcini.

96 'I CAN'T TELL WHY, BUT SO IT IS' Source: *Bouts-Rimés and Noun Verses*, p. 29.
A mile of open JEAL is referring to hunting of course.

97 'TO LEARN TO DANCE' Source: *Bouts-Rimés and Noun Verses*, p. 30.

97 'BETWEEN THE RED ROSE AND THE WHITE' Source: *Bouts-Rimés and Noun Verses*, p. 31.
the Red Rose and the White Emblems of respectively the Lancastrians and the Yorkists in the Wars of the Roses.

98 'SAYS MR. PARROT UNTO ME' Source: Mary Augusta Austen-Leigh,

James Edward Austen Leigh: A Memoir, p. 161.

Mr. *Parrot* James Leigh-Perrot (1735-1817) was the brother of Mrs George Austen.

98 'BETWEEN THE GNAT OR BUTTERFLY' Source: Mary Augusta Austen-Leigh, *James Edward Austen Leigh: A Memoir*, p. 161.

the "Cornhill" The monthly periodical founded in 1860 and first edited by Thackeray.

the "Monthly Packet" A monthly magazine, evangelical in tone, founded in 1851 and first edited by Charlotte M. Yonge. Its full title was *The Monthly Packet of Evening Reading for Younger Members of the English Church*.

98 'THE CASE LIES IN AN EGGSHELL' Source: Gilson MS.

an Eggshell A small measure of quantity (cf. 'in a nutshell').

99 'DISTRESSING THOUGHT! WHERE – WHERE -- WHO KNOWS'
Source: *Bouts-Rimés and Noun Verses*, p. 33.

Jael's tent In Judges IV, Jael, the wife of Heber, kills Sisera, captain of the Canaanite army, by hammering a tent nail into his temples.

the "Boar's Head" The tavern in 1 and 2 *Henry IV* frequented by Falstaff and his companions.

99 'AS SELDOM TAKE I SNUFF, ALACK!' Source: *Bouts-Rimés and Noun Verses*, p. 35.

Robert Possibly Robert Jocock, whipper-in to Sir John Cope and from 1853 to 1865 huntsman of the Garth Hounds, which succeeded Sir John's.

100 'YOU ASK ME WHY COCK A DOODLE DOES CROW?' Source: Gilson MS.

INDEX OF FIRST LINES

Alas! Brother reynard the races are over	13
And art thou come once more to see a Spot	43
And have I written since the earliest ray	53
Anna, this little flowret take	23
Are then my dreams of self importance o'er	77
As seldom take I snuff, alack!	99
Between the Gnat or Butterfly	98
Between the Red Rose and the White	97
Dear Anna look, and you will see	21
Distressing thought! Where – where – who knows	99
Faint echoes of departed verse	94
First rising at mom l enquire with care	14
Fishing tadpoles from a ditch	93
Hard is the task which you have laid	33
Hark, from each sacred Turret's ivied Tower	47
Hark! where those shadowy woodlands sleep	91
Here lies than whom a better hound	50
Here, mid the Flock his fond attention fed	64
How thick on the heraldic page	92
I ask not the aid of Pamassus's quire	49
I can' t tell why, but so it is	96
I tied up my leg	93
If merits should he rightly reckoned	96
In days of yore, when 'Prentice gay	91
In Venta's consecrated Pile	58
Kind neighbours and friends I've a secret to tell	83
Let Harmsworth display on her long Kennel Wall	81
Me impsh it omp a toimsbud	20
Mirror of Life! where lie confus'dly tost	73
"Moses, stand forth! confess thy power now vain	54
My dear, I'm sure your end of town	95
My dearest Friend you bid me write	29
My Father, to whose constant care thy boy	25
My 1st. is of nature, my 2d of art	87
My 1st. is oft done by old persons & Boys	87
My 1st should be long	89
My 1st. tho' now no chicken thought	90

My first, to aid the works of Man 88

My grateful thanks, my Mother dear 9

My Lectures o'er, my Books packd up 67

November's blasts are rough & rude 36

No words can express my dear Aunt my surprise 27

Nine are gone, the tenth appears 45

Ω Δυχε, –– ω φιλολογε 65

"Oh: Betty what makes me look such a fright?" 91

Oh! dear I am sure I don't know what to do 76

Poor neck of Veal, dont pity me 7

Says Mr. Parrot unto me 98

Shake my 1st., & to you in return it will give 88

Some one must pay for every whistle 93

Soon as was known in great Dean Town 10

Sweet Manydown, thou scene of Pleasures past 31

Theyve fixed on the place, for the new 'pointed race 12

The case lies in an Eggshell 98

They who have climbed the steep ascent of power 92

Though superstitious folk may say 8

To learn to dance 97

To your letter, dear Anna. though hard-pressed for time 62

Well I remember, once Papa 17

What does that fair girl's heart commemorate 94

What when the golden Age was gone 86

When first the Fox the lion saw 28

When the sailor boy rocked on the boundless pacific 79

Where are those Men? say Tyrant where 19

Whilst I am toiling here in vain 22

William, A Muse I once possesed 74

With victories of every kind 94

Ye Nymphs of Chawion to my lay attend 85

Yes lady to his promise just 38

Yes still the same, though Priams Towers fall 52

Yes thou art Grandieurs self thou Nature's boast 40

You ask me why Cock a doodle does crow? 100

Tour hounds are much too fresh and gay 91

Also published by the Jane Austen Society

Collected Reports 1949 – 1965
Collected Reports 1966 – 1975
Collected Reports 1976 – 1985
Collected Reports 1986 – 1995
Collected Reports 1996 – 2000
(includes index for 1949 – 2000

Godmersham Park, by Nigel Nicolson
Jane Austen in Bath, by Jean Freeman
My Aunt, Jane Austen: a memoir, by Caroline Austen
Reminiscences of Caroline Austen, ed. Deirdre Le Faye
Jane Austen in Lyme Regis, by Maggie Lane
Fanny Knight's Diaries, ed. Deirdre Le Faye
The Complete Poems of James Austen, ed David Selwyn

In association with Carcanet Press
JaneAusten: Collected Poems and verse of the
Austen family, ed. David Selwyn
Jane Austen: A Celebration,
ed. Maggie Lane and David Selwyn